MARLOWE
AND HIS CIRCLE

Marlowe
AND HIS CIRCLE

A Biographical Survey

by

Frederick S. Boas

M.A. (Oxon.); Hon. LL.D. (St. Andrews)

OXFORD
At the CLARENDON PRESS
1929

OXFORD UNIVERSITY PRESS
Amen House, E.C. 4
London   Edinburgh   Glasgow
Leipzig   New York   Toronto
Melbourne   Capetown   Bombay
Calcutta   Madras   Shanghai
HUMPHREY MILFORD
Publisher to the
University

Printed in Great Britain

Preface

IN the pages that follow my first aim has been to take stock of the documentary materials for the biography of Christopher Marlowe and his associates that have been brought to light during the present century. The subject is one that has specially interested me since I printed, nearly thirty years ago, in *The Fortnightly Review* and afterwards in the Introduction to my edition of Thomas Kyd's works, a letter of Kyd to Sir John Puckering describing his relations with Marlowe. Since then new biographical materials have accumulated, especially those contained in Dr. Leslie Hotson's notable volume, *The Death of Christopher Marlowe* (1925), which has stimulated further criticism and investigation.

For the most part these new contributions to our knowledge have appeared as articles or letters in magazines and periodicals English, American, and foreign. It may therefore be of service to attempt to survey them briefly as a whole, and to interpret them in their relation to one another and to our previous sources of information.

In this light I have sought, as my second aim, to reconsider the case for and against accepting the verdict of the Coroner's jury that Ingram Frizer killed 'Christopher Morley' on 30 May 1593 in self-defence. Miss Ellis-Fermor in her *Christopher Marlowe* (1927) sums up what is the prevalent attitude of Elizabethan scholars when she declares that the narrative of the eye-witnesses 'seems to have satisfied the sixteen jurors; it is far from satisfying Marlowe's present-day biographers, among whom there is a prevailing impression that he was deliberately murdered'. I have quoted typical criticisms of the jury's verdict, but have tried to show that it is consistent with what we hear from his contemporaries about Marlowe's conduct and personality.

In considering the question, account has of course to be taken of the three companions of Marlowe on the fatal 30 May. To Dr. Hotson and to Miss E. de Kalb we are indebted for what we know about Frizer and his companion Skeres. But I have been able to trace the career of Robert Poley in more detail than has been hitherto done, and to give reasons for regarding him as the most important of the three witnesses. I have not attempted to conceal the fact that his testimony must be treated as suspect, and that this must weigh *pro tanto* against our acceptance of the jury's verdict.

The greater part of Chapter II, in which Poley's earlier career is discussed, appeared in *The Nineteenth Century and After*, October, 1928, but I have made additions and corrections, and the extracts from the State Papers are now given in their original spelling though contractions are expanded.

I have drawn attention also to recently published letters concerning the Italian musician, Alfonso Ferrabosco, whose employment

7

as an agent by Elizabeth's government affords something of a parallel to Marlowe's temporary service in State affairs.

I have not attempted any synthesis between the documentary materials and impressions about Marlowe's character and opinions drawn from his plays and poems. Such a synthesis is, of course, legitimate and indeed necessary for a 'full-dress' biography, but I hope that a useful end may be attained by a more objective treatment.[1]

July 1929.   F. S. B.

---

[1] As these pages go to press, a valuable article on 'Marlowe, Robert Poley and the Tippings' by Miss Ethel Seaton has appeared in *The Review of English Studies* (July). Further researches by Miss de Kalb, embodied in an academic thesis, have not yet been published.

Contents

List of Illustrations

I have to thank Mr. D. McL. Wheeler of King's School, Canterbury, who (through the courtesy of the Head Master, Mr. N. P. Birley) took the photograph of the recently completed Marlowe Memorial, on the Dane John, Canterbury, which is reproduced, in reduced size, on the jacket of this volume.

CHAPTER ONE

Canterbury and Cambridge

§ The Three Christopher Morleys

ASURVEY of the documentary sources for the career of Christopher Marlowe may begin with the record of the marriage of his parents in the 'Register Booke' of the Parish of St. George the Martyr, Canterbury, under the date 22 May, 1561, 'John Marlowe and Catherine Arthur'.[1] The father was a member of the shoemakers and tanners' guild of the city; the mother appears to have been the daughter of Christopher Arthur, rector of the Church of St. Peter's, 1550–52. The first child of the marriage, Mary, daughter of John Marlowe, was christened at St. George's on 21 May, 1562. On 6 February, 156¾, the eldest son was born, and on 26 February he was christened as 'Christofer the sonne of

[1] *The Register Booke of the Parish of St. George the Martyr within the Citie of Canterburie*, ed. by J. M. Cowper.

11

John Marlow'. Two months later, according to the Canterbury city records, on 20
April, 'John M'lyn of Canter. Shomaker,
was admitted and sworn to ye lib'ty of y^s
Citte for ye whitche he pd but iiii^s. i^d be-
caus he was inrowlyd w'thy^n y^s citte acord-
ing to ye customes of ye same'. The dramatist's father, who was already inscribed on
the burgess rolls, thus took up his full citizen-
ship at the customary reduced fee. He appears at a later period to have taken on the
duties of a parish clerk. There is an entry
in the register book of St. George the Martyr
on 26 January 160$\frac{4}{5}$ of the death of 'John
Marloe, clark of St. Maries'.

On 14 January 15$\frac{78}{79}$ Christopher was admitted to one of the scholarships for boys between
the ages of nine and fifteen at the ancient
King's School. His name appears as Chr[ist]o-
fer Marley in the treasurer's accounts of payments made to the scholars in 1578–9. The
accounts for the following year are missing.
Owing to the late age at which he entered his
stay at the school was short, only about two
years. But it probably helped to quicken his
dramatic interests. The publication of the
History of the King's School, Canterbury, by
Messrs. Woodruff and Cape (1908) has shown

Chap. I
Canterbury and Cambridge

that the school was a centre of theatrical activities in Elizabethan times and later, and that the Dean and Chapter contributed liberally to the setting forth by 'the schoolmaster and scholars' of tragedies, comedies, and interludes.

It will be noted that the variant spellings of the dramatist's surname, which have added to the problems of his biography, begin to appear in the Canterbury documents. His father's name is 'Marlowe' or 'Marlow' in the marriage and baptismal entries, 'M[ar]lyn' when he is admitted as a freeman, and 'Marloe' when he is buried; 'Marley' is the boy's designation as a King's School scholar. When he went up to Cambridge he appears to have been known at first as 'Marlin' or 'Marlen'. The list of matriculations in the University Registry, under the date 17 March 158$\frac{0}{1}$, includes 'Coll. corp. x^r. Chrof. Marlen'. He is entered among the 'Pensioners' as Marlin in the college admission book (*Registrum Parvum*), his name being the last but one in 1580, i.e. before 25 March 158$\frac{0}{1}$, and this is the almost uniform spelling of his name in the college documents till Michaelmas, 1585. He is also 'Marlin' in the supplicat for his B.A. degree

in March 158¾. But the entry in the Grace
Book of that date has 'Marley', which is
also the form in his supplicat for the M.A.
in 1587 and the corresponding entry in
the Grace Book. The college accounts in
1586–7 have 'Marly' and 'Marlye'. This
form seems, therefore, to have got the better
of 'Marlin' in his later Cambridge years, and
by it or its variant 'Morley' he would be
likely to be known outside the University.

For these details, and for any further information about Marlowe's Cambridge life,
we are chiefly indebted to an article by Professor Moore Smith in *The Modern Language
Review* (January, 1909). Dr. Moore Smith
has made a detailed examination of the Corpus Christi accounts from 1580 to 1587.
From these it would appear that Marlowe,
though he did not matriculate till 17 March
158°⁄₁, had come into residence early in the
second quarter, or Lent Term. Though admitted as a pensioner, Marlowe drew from
the first an allowance as a scholar. The
scholarship to which he had been nomi-
nated was one of three created by Archbishop Parker's will in 1575. It was restricted
to a native of Canterbury educated at the
King's School. The allowance was 'juxta

xii^d in septimana pro rata residentiæ cuiusque eorum in Collegio'. 'Marlin' received 12 shillings during this quarter, which ended on Lady Day; the two other scholars on the same foundation were paid 13 shillings, so that he appears to have been in residence for all but one week of the term. On 11 May he was formally elected scholar, 'Marlin electus et admissus in locum d[omi]ni Pashley'; and there is an entry in the accounts of his payment of the customary fee on election: 'Marlin, iij^s iiij^d.'

As Marlowe's allowance was 12^d a week it is possible to tell from the payments made to him in each quarter how long he was in residence. The only absences beyond a week or a fortnight before he took his B.A. were in the fourth quarter of 1582, when he drew vij^s, and in the third between Lady Day and Midsummer 1583, when he drew vj^s. During the academic year 1584–5 he was absent more than half the time, the payments in the four terms being respectively iij^s, vij^s vj^d, iiij^s, and v^s. For 1585–6 the accounts are missing.

During the two last quarters of his scholarship in 1586–7 he drew ix^s and v^s vj^d. By Lady Day 1587 he had virtually held

it for the full period of six years, and this
implied, according to Parker's intention, that
he meant to take orders in the Church.

After an uncertain interval—there is a
discrepancy in the records—' Jacobus Bridg-
man electus et admissus est discipulus huius
Collegij in locum Cantuariensis scholaris
vacantem'. In quoting this entry from the
College Order Book, Dr. Moore Smith added:

> 'It is noticeable that the formula of the Or-
> der Book omits Marlowe's name though
> it is usual in such a formula of admission
> that the name of the late holder of the
> scholarship should be stated. Is this an
> indication that Marlowe was in some way
> in bad odour with the College authorities?'

To this question, shrewdly raised in 1909 by
Dr. Moore Smith, an unexpected answer was
to be given in 1925 by Dr. Leslie Hotson
when he drew attention to the following
entry in the Privy Council Register under
the date 29 June 1587, when the Archbishop of Canterbury, the Lord Chancellor,
the Lord Treasurer, the Lord Chamberlain,
and ' Mr. Comptroler' were present:

> ' Whereas it was reported that Christo-
> pher Morley was determined to haue gone
> beyond the seas to Reames and there to

16

remaine   Their Lordships thought good
to certefie that he had no such intent,
but that in all his accions he had behaued
him selfe orderlie and discreetlie where-
bie he had done her Majestie good service,
& deserued to be rewarded for his faith-
full dealinge: Their Lordships request that
the rumor thereof should be allaied by
all possible meanes, and that he should be
furthered in the degree he was to take
this next Commencement: Because it was
not her Majesties pleasure that anie one
emploied as he had been in matters touching the benefitt of his Countrie should
be defamed by those that are ignorant in
th' affaires he went about.'

If the Christopher Morley here mentioned
was the Christopher Marley of the King's
School and the later Cambridge entries, it is
evident that he had got into trouble with
the University authorities, and that the Privy
Council's intervention was necessary to ob-
tain permission for him to proceed to his degree. If this be so, the Council's action had
immediate results. Marlowe's supplicat for
the M.A. was signed by Dr. Robert Norgate,
the Master of his College, and another academic dignitary, and he took the degree in July.

Dr. Hotson's identification of this Christopher Morley with the dramatist has raised
much discussion, and the problem has proved
to be more complex than he thought. He
knew of one other Cambridge Christopher
Morley who had to be considered. This
Morley was a scholar of Trinity, who took
his B.A. in 158$\frac{2}{3}$. As, however, he proceeded
to his M.A. in 1586 he cannot be the man
on whose behalf the Privy Council intervened a year later.

It was natural for Dr. Hotson to conclude
that this Christopher Morley of Trinity was
the Christopher Marlor mentioned in a letter
to the Privy Council by William Vaughan,
written from Pisa on 14 July 1602, 'to fore-
warn the Council of certain caterpillars, I
mean Jesuits and seminary priests, who are
to be sent from the English seminary at Valladolid to pervert and withdraw her Majesty's
loyal subjects from their due obedience to
her . . .'

'In the said seminary there is one Christopher Marlor (as he will be called) but
yet for certainty his name is Christopher,
sometime master in arts of Trinity College
in Cambridge, of very low stature, well set,
of a black round beard, not yet priest, but

to come over in the mission of the next year ensuing.'

But in this identification Dr. Hotson, it has since been proved, was mistaken. There were two, not one, Christopher Morleys or Marlowes at Trinity, Cambridge in the later years of Elizabeth's reign.

Sir Israel Gollancz, in a letter to *The Times*, 23 June 1925, drew attention to the fact that in a document then belonging to Messrs. Dobell, this seminarist Christopher Marlowe is mentioned. The document consists of twenty large folio sheets containing the original bills rendered by the keepers of the Gatehouse Prison, Westminster, for the diet and other necessaries of prisoners from 1596–1606. On the sheet containing the bills from 25 June 1604 to 23 Sept. 1604 the following entry is found:

Committed by my Lorde Cheife Justice	Christopher Marlowe *alias* Mathews, a seminary preist owith for his dyet & lodging for 7 weeks, and two days being close prisoner at the rate of 14^s the weeke 5^{li} 2^s For washinge 2^{s}4^d ... £5. 4^s 4^d.

Sir Israel was right in identifying this 'Mar-

lowe *alias* Mathews' with the Marlor mentioned by Vaughan. But he was mistaken,
as has been since proved, in going on to
identify him also with the Christopher Morley 'in furtherance of whose degree, the
Privy Council drew up the certificate in
1587'—in which case, of course, there
would have been no question of its referring
to Marlowe the dramatist. A month later,
in a letter to *The Times*, July 24, Mr. J. B.
Whitmore from inquiries made at Valladolid
was able to show that the seminarist could
not have been alluded to in the Privy Council entry. The records of the English College show that on 30 May 1599 there was
admitted to the college John Matthew
(Mathews) *alias* Christopher Marler, aged
twenty-seven, born and educated at Cambridge where he spent seven years at Trinity
College, and had taken his B.A. and M.A.
He was converted by Father Thomas Wright,
and received into the Roman Catholic Church
by Father Garnett, S.J., and had been im-
prisoned in the Clink for fifteen days before he left England.

From the University records it appears
that this John Mathews came up to Trinity
from Westminster School in Michaelmas

1588 (when he was about sixteen), took his
B A. in 1592/3, and his M.A. in 1596. He
was therefore still at Westminster when the
Privy Council certificate was issued.

He was consecrated priest in September
1602, and was sent back to England in the
spring of 1603. It was he who, as the documents concerning the Gatehouse Prison show,
was arrested in the summer of 1604, and
was afterwards deported.

Thus the progress of investigation since
Dr. Hotson's book was published, while it
has corrected details in his views, has gone
far to confirm his main conclusion that the
Christopher Morley on whose behalf the
Privy Council intervened was the Morley
or Marlowe of Corpus Christi College, and
that he had been engaged on some government service during one of the periods of his
absence from Cambridge after taking his B.A.,
perhaps the months after his last scholarship payment, between February and June
1587.

During this period he had been 'defamed
by those that are ignorant in th' affaires he
went about'. This defamation Dr. Hotson
interprets vaguely, 'by turning the Council's language inside out', as a report that 'he

was disorderly in his behaviour and indis-
creet in his actions'. He seems to me here
to have missed the full significance of part
of his own discovery. I believe that the key
is in the opening words of the entry in the
Council's register: 'Whereas it was reported
that Christopher Morley was determined to
haue gone beyond the seas to Reames and
there to remaine Their Lordships thought
good to certefie that he had no such intent.'
For ' busy tongues ' to give out (in Dr. Hotson's paraphrase) that ' he was to go to Rheims
for a protracted stay ' is not on the face of
it a damning allegation. But let us turn for
illumination to Part I of *The Return from
Parnassus*, v. iii, 1585–6. Here the two Cambridge scholars, Studiosus and Philomusus, in
despair of making a living at home decide to
fly to foreign climes, ' to Rome or Rheims '
apparently in the hope of being rewarded by
the Roman Catholic Church as fugitives from
England and likely converts. Was not this
the sting in the allegation? Did not Marlowe's enemies suggest in 1587, as they did
later in 1593, that he had leanings towards
Roman Catholicism, almost as deadly a charge
at the time as the alternative accusation
against him of atheism?

It has to be remembered that Rheims and
Rome had taken the place of Douai and Louvain as the head-quarters of English Roman Catholics on the Continent. The English College at Douai, founded by the Pope at his own expense, had been closed by the new governor of the city and province in March 1578, and its members had to take refuge at Rheims. The importance attached by the Holy See to the welfare of the college in its new home is shown in a letter from the Papal Secretary of State to the Nuncio in France, dated 19 May 1578. After mentioning the expulsion from Douai he continues:

'And whereas Dr. Allen, Rector of that College, a man most exemplary and good and learned, has thereby been constrained to withdraw with his comrades to the city of Reims in that realm, therefore it has seemed good to the Pope that they make their abode there to continue their work: and so, while providing them with money, he has warmly commended them to the Cardinal of Reims and the Chapter of the said church, that they may be accorded all needful aid and favour. And as it is feared that the pretended Queen of England who shows herself most ill disposed towards the said Dr. Allen will do her utmost with his Most Christian Majesty to procure his and his comrade's expulsion from the realm of France, even as they have been expelled from the province of Flanders, his Holiness has charged me to write to you bidding you to exhort and beseech his said Majesty not only to allow them to abide in the realm and in that city of Reims, but also to direct that they be well treated, and accorded the favour of residing there in security and peace of mind, whereby his Majesty, besides sharing in the merit of so worthy a wish, will do a thing in the last degree acceptable to the Pope.'[1]

At Rome as early as 1575–6 an assembly of English Roman Catholic exiles, headed by Sir Richard Shelley and Sir Thomas Stucley, had promoted a scheme for the invasion of England which was favoured by Gregory XIII, but which found at the time a lukewarm supporter in Philip II. Elizabeth retaliated by making use for her own purposes of Italians in England. And the

[1] *Calendar of State Papers relating to English Affairs, preserved principally at Rome,* vol. ii, 1572–1578, p. 435, ed. J. M. Rigg (1926).

publication in 1926 of Vatican documents
for 1572–8 has opportunely revealed the
unsuspected political activities of an Italian
musician who has hitherto seemed as remote
as Marlowe, the playwright, from affairs
of state. Alfonso Ferrabosco the eldest, of
Bologna, had been domiciled in England at
least as early as 1562 when he was granted
an annuity of 100 marks. He is mentioned
in the Revels Accounts in connexion with
a masque in June 1572 and a play in February 1576, and was a composer of airs
and madrigals. Sir Edmund Chambers has
pointed out (*Elizabethan Stage*, i. 256) that
he was in all probability the Bolognese
groom of the privy chamber favoured by
Elizabeth as an excellent musician who
suggested to some Venetian visitors in 1575
the desirability of a Venetian embassy in
London.

But a letter from the Nuncio in Paris to
the Papal Secretary of State, dated 23 June
1578, shows that Elizabeth used his services
not only as an excellent musician but as an
agent in state affairs.

'There has arrived here one Alfonso
Ferrabosco of Bologna, brought hither
by the Cardinal of Lorraine as his

musician. Determined against the will of his father to serve the Queen of England, he had been there for many years, requited with favour and pay. But at length it being alleged that he had gone to Mass in the house of the ambassador of France, he was forbidden access to the Queen's chambers and the Court. He has visited me, and told me that though he is now reinstated in his office and the favour of his Patroness, he has resolved to be quit of that servitude, and acknowledge his error, and go home to Italy; and that he has taken occasion of the death of his mother to crave leave of absence for a few months, purposing not to return. And so he besought my advice, and also letters of recommendation to procure him pardon of his error, and enable him to live at home as a good Catholic and Christian . . . I commended his professed resolution denouncing the servitude; and I exhorted him to go at once to the Pope without trepidation . . .

'I understand that this is a most evil-spirited, evil-minded man, and very knowing, and excellently informed of the affairs of those countries; that the Queen of England makes such use of him as a spy and complotter, in which character he might now be employed, so that if one had him in one's power, one might learn many things; that it is in order that he may better play his game that he affects to have a grudge against the Queen of England; and that therefore he will go to Italy, and in particular to Rome and Bologna. I know not what of good to believe, as here he has gone to dine with the ambassador of England on Friday, and has eaten meat, and is constantly busy there ... I have placed persons about him to try if they can penetrate his mind, and I will apprise you of the result.'[1]

Three days later the Nuncio adds that though Ferrabosco affects to be incensed against the Queen of England he had from her 'a present of 8,000 crowns on his departure, and is taking with him two jennets to bestow in Italy on two persons of quality who are at her service for this turn.'[2] In spite of the Nuncio's suspicions Ferrabosco would appear to have made his home again in Italy—nothing more is known of him in England—and to have gained favour later at the Court of Savoy. In publishing a book

[1] *op. cit.*, pp. 458–9. [2] *op. cit.*, p. 461.

of madrigals at Venice in September, 1587,
he signs himself 'gentil' huomo dell' Altezza
di Savoia'.

This new light upon the double career of
Ferrabosco as a musician and a political
agent helps us to realize Marlowe in a similarly double rôle of dramatist and government servant. Moreover, the equivocal conduct which the Nuncio attributes to Ferrabosco, and his own double-faced dealing with
him, go far to demonstrate how, in this sub-
terranean sphere of moves and countermoves,
Marlowe might nine years later be accused,
with or without some warrant, of having
contemplated flight to Rome or Rheims.
And we are even encouraged to hope that
some archive at home or abroad may yet
reveal the nature of his secret service in or
before 1587.

Meanwhile, it must be a matter of conjecture whether this service brought Marlowe
during his Cambridge days into contact with
a man who was even more deeply involved
than Ferrabosco as a 'spy and complotter'
in the intrigues preceding and following the
execution of Mary, Queen of Scots, and with
whom the dramatist was to be associated in
the last fatal crisis of his life. Whenever

their connexion began, it is of first-rate im- portance for the biography of Marlowe to trace, as far as possible, the turbulent career of Robert Poley.

CHAPTER TWO

Robert Poley

¶ Prisoner, Spy, and 'Complotter',
1583–1589

IN attempting to follow up the clues to
Robert Poley's career we are faced with
the same difficulties of Elizabethan no-
menclature as in the case of Marlowe himself. His name, as has been seen, has such
variants as 'Marlin', 'Marley', and 'Morley'. So Poley appears as 'Pooley', 'Poole',
and 'Pole', and allusions to him in the
State Papers are indexed in the Calendars
under these various names, as if they referred to different persons. On the other
hand, as there were two other contemporary
Christopher Morleys in addition to the
dramatist, there may have been more than
one Robert Poley, though the extant references all appear to fit the same man. There
is greater difficulty when, as often happens,
allusions are made to Poley or Poole without
a Christian name. These are equivocal and
must be judged on their merits. Thus as Robert

Poley or Poole was with Marlowe on 30
May 1593, it is reasonable to conclude that
he is identical with 'one Poole, a prisoner
in newgate' with whom, according to a
Note delivered by Richard Baines on Whitsun Eve, 2 June 1593,[1] Marlowe was acquainted, and who had taught him how to
counterfeit French and English coinage.
If the identification is correct, Baines's allegation is of considerable importance, as the
only link, outside of the legal records, between Marlowe and any of the three companions of his last hours, Robert Poley,
Ingram Frizer, and Nicholas Skeres.

Though he cannot have been in Newgate
at the date of Marlowe's death, Poley had
often been in confinement. The first record
that we have of him is as a prisoner. In
January 158$\frac{8}{9}$ he was involved in some remarkable proceedings (of which more here-
after) for alienating the affections of Joan the
wife of William Yeomans, a London Cutler.[2]

Among the deponents in the case before

---

[1] See below, p. 71.
[2] The brief headings in *The Calendar of State Papers*
(*Domestic*) under the date 7 Jan. 158$\frac{8}{9}$ do not suffi-
ciently indicate the value of the depositions in their
full form for Poley's biography.

William Fleetwood, the Recorder, was Richard Ede, apparently lodgekeeper at the Marshalsea; whose knowledge of Poley went back to 1583. On a date not specified in that year, according to Ede, Poley was committed by Sir Francis Walsingham to the Marshalsea and remained there till the 10th of May following. One half of the time he was a close prisoner; and the other half he had 'the liberty of the house'. He made use of this 'enlargement' to entertain Mistress Yeomans at 'fine bankets' in his chamber, while refusing to have anything to do with his own wife, who often tried to see him. This ill-used lady (as we learn from Yeomans) was 'one Watson's daughter', and was married to Poley by a seminary priest in the house of one Wood, a tailor dwelling in Bow Lane, who circulated prohibited books like *The Execution of Justice*, and *The Treatise of Schism*.

Whatever the reason for Poley's committal to the Marshalsea, he cannot have been in want of money at this time, for he entrusted Mistress Yeomans with £110 of 'good gould'. After a time he sent Mistress Ede to borrow £3 from Yeomans, who was not at home. Mistress Yeomans, however,

sent him back by the messenger £3 of his
own money. Yeomans afterwards sent by
his brother another £3, and when mistress
Ede declared that the money had already
been received by Poley, Yeomans thought
his wife had robbed him and was angry with
her. But when Poley came out of prison,
the matter was explained and Ede brought
about a reconciliation, confirmed by a gift
of Poley to Yeomans of a silver buckle
double gilt, and to Ede of two angels for his
pains in the matter. But the intrigue between
Poley and Joan Yeomans continued, and to
facilitate it she arranged for him to have
a chamber at the house of her mother, a
widowed mistress Browne.

Apparently, however, mistress Browne did
not suspect the guilty relations between her
daughter and Poley, which had a remarkable sequel. One of the deponents who gave
evidence before the Recorder on 7 January
$158\frac{8}{9}$ was Agnes Hollford, wife of Ralph
Hollford, hosier. She deposed that on a Friday about Shrovetide, 1585, she met mistress Browne, mother of mistress Yeomans.
Mistress Browne told her that ' one Mr.
Polley laye in her howse, and her daughter
comminge to her howse to drye clothes '

she 'fownde her daughter sittinge vpon the
said Polleys knees, the syght thereof did soe
stryke to her hart that she shoulde never
recover yt. She prayed God to cutt her of
verie quickly or ells she feared she shoulde
be a bawde vnto her owne daughter.' Her
prayer was quickly answered, for when mistress Hollford called on mistresse Browne on
the Monday following she found her 'de-
parted and readie to be caried to the Church
to be buried, she dyinge vppon the Sater-
daie before'. Even this divine visitation,
however, did not, as will be seen, put a stop
to the relations between Poley and mistress
Yeomans.

By 1585, however, Poley had become associated with a very different circle from
that of the London cutler and his wife.
Charles and Christopher Blunt (or Blount)
were younger brothers of William, seventh
Lord Mountjoy. Charles, who was a favour-
ite of Elizabeth, succeeded to the title in
1594, and afterwards became Earl of Devon-
shire and Lord Deputy of Ireland. Christopher was Master of the Horse to Lord
Leicester, whose widow he married about
1589. He was knighted for his military
services in Flanders in 1587-8. He after-

34

wards took part in the ill-fated campaign of the Earl of Essex in Ireland, and in the abortive conspiracy against Elizabeth, for which he was executed on 18 March 1601. This was the culmination of a long series of treasonable practices. By 1585 Christopher Blunt, who became a convert to Roman Catholicism, had thrown himself ardently into the plots on behalf of the unfortunate Queen of Scots. For this purpose he chose as his agent Robert Poley, as appears to be first mentioned in a letter from Thomas Morgan to Mary, dated 10 July 1585. Morgan, one of Mary's agents abroad, was at this time a prisoner in the Bastille, but he was able to communicate in cipher with the Queen of Scots, then at Tutbury in the custody of Sir Amias Poulet.

'Aboute fiftene dayes past or thereaboutes, there arrived here a speciall messenger from London, sent hither expresselye by Mr. Blunt vnto me with letters, declaring by the same that he was bound to serve & honor the only Sainct that he knowes living vppon the grownd—so he termed your majestie . . . which bringer of Blunt his letters is a gentleman & named Robert Poley. I am, as I was, still prisonner

& he cold not be permitted to have ac-
cesse vnto me.'

Poley, however, refused to deal with Morgan through any intermediary, 'declaring
that he wold not deliver his charge to none
living till he spake with my selfe or hard
me speak'. Some of Morgan's friends became
apprehensive, beginning 'to dout the sayd
Poley was sent by England to practise my
death in prison by one meanes or other'.
Morgan, however, was not influenced by
their fears :

'I fownd the meanes to have him con-
ducted as nere as might be to the window
of the chamber where I am a prisoner,
and through the window I spoke so moch
to him as satisfied him, who at the last delivered the letters where I appoynted, &
so they came to my handes with ample
Instrucions of the state of England . . .

And so vppon conference and conclusion
with the sayd Poley I fownd nothing but
that he ment well, and a Catholike he
showeth himselfe to be, and moch disposed to see some happye & speedye re-
formation in that state . . . I have retorned
Poley in fine well contented and con-

firmed, I hope, to serve your majestie in
all he may, but I wrote not one line with
him, but signified that Blunt shold heare
from me by some other meanes.'

The last words suggest that Morgan did
not trust Poley fully, but in any case he got
him recompensed for 'his viage and charges
hither'. He persuaded the Archbishop of
Glasgow to send Poley 30 pistolets through
Charles Paget.

'He hath received the same, & is gone
to England wher he promised Paget to
do some good offices, & prayed him to
assure me thereof, for I cold not be permitted to speak with him but once, as I
tolde you alredye.'

Morgan's caution in not communicating
with Blount through Poley proved fruitless.
For as Charles Paget, another fervent ad-
herent in Paris of the Queen of Scots, wrote
to Mary on July 15, Poley himself on his
first arrival there 'committed an error in
writing hence to Mr. Christopher Blunt'
and 'sent it by an ordinary messenger, so
that it was taken'. This is confirmed on
July 18 by Morgan, 'I hear that the said
Poleys letters were intercepted at the port

in England and sent to the Council'. In all probability Poley did not ' commit an error' but deliberately arranged that the correspondence should fall into the hands of the English Government.[1]

Exactly six months afterwards, on 18 January 1586, Morgan gives further news of Poley :

' Hert [i.e. Charles Paget] and I recommend the French Embassador some English in London to doe him some pleasure & service there and amongst others one Robert Poley who hath geven me assurance to serve and honor your majestie to his power being but a poore gentleman. He is moch at Chr[istopher] Blunt his devotion and both of them do travell to make an intelligence for your majestie. The sayd Embassador & his Secretarye

[1] In the Autumn of 1585 Poley seems to have visited Denmark. On October 16 Thomas Tenneker, draper, writes to Walsingham from 'Hellsingnour'. 'On 19 September two English gentlemen Pooley and Sandey arrived. The King entertaineth them both in service. They have but a hundred dollars fee and 16 dollars apiece for board wages. I think they do it in order, when they will, to be at liberty to pass further, with the King's passport' (*Calendar of State Papers (Foreign)*, September 1585—May 1586).

Courdaillot have sithence theyr arrivall
in London reported well to Hert and to
my selfe of the sayd Poley who hath bene
heretofore in Scotland & knoweth the
best wayes to passe into Scotlande. If you
know not how to be better served for
conveyance to Scotland you may cause
the Embassador to addresse the sayd Poley
with your letters into Scotland. But order
must be taken to make his charges in such
viages. And if your majestie will have
him to remayne in some place nerer for
your purpose & service he will accom-
modate himself accordinglye to your pleasure. He is a Catholike and Blunt has
placed him to be Sir Phillipp Sydneys man
that he may more quietlye live a Christian
life vnder the sayd Sydney.'

What an exquisite compliment to the *preux
chevalier* of the Elizabethan age (though
the Calendar of the Scottish State Papers
cynically omits it)! But it was of course not
with Poley's progress in the religious life
that Mary's supporters were concerned.
They secured him a place in Sidney's service because on 20 September 1583 Sir
Philip had married Frances, daughter of Sir
Francis Walsingham, and had taken up his

abode in his father-in-law's house. Poley
would thus be in a favourable position for
learning 'Mr. Secretary's' movements and
plans.

In a later letter to the Queen of Scots,
dated 21 March 1586, Morgan states this
without any disguise:

'Having written thus farre I receaved letters out of England from London from
Poley, in my former letters mentioned,
who writeth vnto me that he hath bene
in the partes where your majesty remayneth, and there addressed the meanes to
convey such letters as I commended to his
care to serve to make an intelligence with
your majesty. We have applyed him this
twelve monthe or thereabouts & have
fownd him to deale well & verye willing to serve your majesty. Hert can tell
yow he was first recommended vnto me
by Christopher Blunt who never abused
[i. e. deceived] me, but continueth well
affected to serve & honor your majesty.
And I am of opinion that you entertayne
the sayd Poley who by Bluntes labours
& my advise is placed with the Ladye
Sydney, the dowghter of Secretarye Walsingham, & by that means ordinarilye

in his Howse and therebye able to picke
owt many things to the information of
your majesty. Blunt & he in favour of
your majesty & by my instigation have
done acceptable service to the French
Embassador at his first arrivall in England, whenas he was so narrowlye loked
into as fewe or none of the English durst
approch his howse, moch less conferre
with him or any of his. . . . . As I have
sayd, [Poley] is in a place to discover
many thinges which he beginneth to doe
to the disadvantage of the common enemies.'

Morgan goes on to tell Mary that 'eyther
Rawley, the mignon of her of England is
wearye of her or els she is wearye of him,
for I heare she hath now entertayned one
[Charles] Blunt, brother of the Lord Mount-
joye, a yong gentilman, whose grand-
mother she may be for her age and his'.
It is therefore expedient that Mary should
make Poley understand that she thinks well
of this gentleman's brother, Christopher,
'who is at present in Holland with Leicester, & has sent for Poley to come to him'.
There is no evidence as to whether or not
Poley obeyed this summons. But on 10 April,

Charles Paget wrote, as Morgan had done ten days before, emphasizing the advantage to Mary's cause of Poley's position in Sidney's service.

'There be two other which be in practyse to gayne others to serve your majesty for intelligence, whereof one is called Poley, a great friend to Christopher Blunt, of whome I suppose your majesty hath harde here tofore. Morgan and I have had conference with the sayd Poley and hope he is in soch place, being servant to Sir Phillipp Sydney, and thereby remayneth with his Ladye and in house with Secretarye Walsingham, so as he shalbe able to give your majesty advertisement from time to time.'

As Sir Philip had left England on 16 November 1585, to take up his post as Governor of Flushing, and as he remained in the Netherlands till his death on 17 October 1586, Poley can have had little personal intercourse with him. But as both Morgan and Paget state, he remained with Lady Sidney, who followed her husband about the end of March. His employment in Sir Francis Walsingham's house suggests various links and is of importance for the biography of Marlowe. It was at Scadbury, the Chislehurst estate of Thomas Walsingham, son of a cousin of Sir Francis, that the Privy Council on 18 May 1593 ordered their messenger to seek out Marlowe for arrest. Ingram Frizer, who killed Marlowe, and with whom Skeres was in close league, was in the service of Thomas Walsingham. Poley, as his own words will show, while acting as an agent for Sir Francis, was brought into direct association with Thomas Walsingham, who thus appears as the centre of the group. It may well have been at his Chislehurst home, or at one of the two residences of 'Mr. Secretary', in London or at Barn Elms, that Marlowe and Poley first met. If their association began as early as 1587, when (as Dr. Moore Smith has shown) there was a break in Marlowe's Cambridge residence, and when (as Dr. Hotson discovered) he was employed 'in matters touching the benefit of his country', this would throw light on an obscure passage in his career. It would help to account for the report that Marlowe intended to go beyond the seas to Rheims and to remain at that centre of Roman Catholic propaganda—a report against which the Privy Council protested so ener-

43

getically, when in June 1587 they ordered
that he should be furthered in the degree
that he was to take 'this next Commencement' at Cambridge. In any case Poley's
equivocal activities illustrate how easily Marlowe might have been employed by the authorities in matters touching the benefit of
his country which would lend themselves to
misrepresentation. And an episode, which
if William Yeomans's memory on 7 January
1589 is to be trusted, took place early in
1586, throws a remarkable light on Poley's
mentality. 'About three years past' according to Yeomans, Poley was examined before
Sir Francis Walsingham 'by the space of
two hours touching a book which was made
against the Earl of Leicester.' This was evidently the notorious *Leicester's Commonwealth*, published in 1584, and prohibited
by the Privy Council on 28 June 1585.

'Although Mr. Secretary did vse him very
cruelly [? put him to the torture] yet woulde
he never confes ytt. And he saied that he
putt Mr. Secretary into that heate that he
looked out of his wyndowe and grynned like
a dogge.' Yeomans asked Poley how he 'durst
to denye the having of the said booke because he verie well knewe that he had the

44

same.'[1] 'Marye', answered Poley, 'it is noe matter for I will sweare and forsweare my selffe rather then I will accuse my selffe to doe me any harme.' What an avowal from one of the trio on whose evidence the coroner's jury were to be dependent later for their verdict on how Marlowe met his death!

During the summer of 1586 Poley was becoming more and more deeply involved in plots and counterplots. He wrote an unsigned letter of thanks to Mary, Queen of Scots, which evidently caused her some perplexity. She refers on July 27 to 'a letter of Poleyes as I judge by reason of some reward he thanketh me for therein receaved

---

[1] One reason for Poley having a copy of *Leicester's Commonwealth* is that he is probably the 'Master Pooley' mentioned on p. 86 (edition of 1641). Lord North was one of those present at the marriage of Leicester to Lettice, Countess of Essex on 21 September 1578, and received in consequence a letter of sharp rebuke from the Queen. According to the writer of *Leicester's Commonwealth* he told 'his trusty Pooly', who repeated the words to Sir Robert Jermine, that 'he was resolved to sinke or swimme with my Lord of Leicester'. If Poley was in the service of Lord North as early as 1578, this would be a sidelight on his career about five years previous to any documentary information.

beyond sea. Otherwise the letter being an unknowne hand without subscription or name therein I am not assured from whence it came. Neyther can I tell by whome to send back my answer agayne.'

Mary had far deeper reason for being distrustful of Poley than she knew. For by July 1586 he had already wormed his way into the secrets of the hot-headed youth, rich and well born, who staked everything for her sake and in losing brought doom upon her as well as himself. Into the well-known story of the conspiracy of Anthony Babington it is not necessary to go here. It is sufficient to say that about April 1586 Babington, largely inspired by John Ballard, a priest from Rheims, formed a plot that included the murder of Elizabeth; that in July he communicated the scheme to Mary; that Ballard was seized early in August; that Babington afterwards fled but was discovered; and that he and Ballard were executed on 20 September. The plot, though completely mismanaged, is of first-rate historical importance because it led directly to Mary's own trial and execution.

Poley's relation to the conspiracy is curiously equivocal. He appears to have been an

agent of Walsingham, but he won Babington's complete confidence, and after the
arrest of the conspirators he was committed
to the Tower, where he was examined on
various charges and made a lengthy confession. From this we learn that he was introduced to Babington in the middle of June,
that he might procure him a licence from
Walsingham for some years of continental
travel:

'I labored . . . that I might accompanye
him betwene the condicyon of a ser-
vaunte & companion beinge vtterly vn-
hable to maintaine myselfe in all this jor-
neye, thinkinge with myselfe that I should
bothe better my selfe thereby bothe in
language and experience and allso do the
State much better servyze in that coursse
abroade then in that wherein I remained
att hoame . . . Babington agreed to supplie
all my charges of travell, and to give me
some yeerly stipende att my retorne . . .
and I tellinge him that I remained bownd
with 2 sureties with me to appear every
20 dayes att the Court, he offered me
£40 or £50 to make means for my discharge, which money I receyved of him
afterwards to that ende the daye before

47

my Lady Sidnies going hence towards Flushinge.'[1]

Here incidentally we get an important side-light on Poley's dubious activities. How was it that he, while in the service of the Sidneys, and in truth with Walsingham, 'remained bownd with two sureties to appear every 20 dayes at the Court', and had to buy his discharge through a gift from Babington? Was it a sequel to his examination concerning *Leicester's Commonwealth*?

Poley procured Babington a couple of interviews with Walsingham, who evidently encouraged further confidences by speaking favourably of the go-between. On Babington's asking by what means Poley's credit grew with Mr. Secretary,

'I towlde him by dealinge with his honor in some busines of my master, Sir Philipp Sidney, but he seeminge to discredite that & urge me further, I towld him further I was in a like coursse of doinge servize to the state as him self had nowe vndertaken. He answered mee that was im-

[1] The dates are difficult to reconcile, for Lady Sidney had gone to Flushing before the middle of June, when, according to Poley, he first met Babington.

possible, because he knew thatt all the
menn of note in England being Catho-
likes had me in vehemente suspicyon.'

For some time longer Poley continued to
play his double part, while Walsingham
made excuses for postponing a further interview with Babington or the grant of his
passport. Then, when all was ready, the
Government struck. Ballard was arrested at
Poley's lodging, immediately after a visit by
Thomas Walsingham 'to whom I had delivered such speeches as Mr. Secretary had
commanded me the day before'. Babington's flight followed, and before his arrest he
wrote Poley a last letter in which affection
and doubt are pathetically mingled:

'I am the same I allwayes pretended. I
pray god yow be, and ever so remayne towardes me. Take hede to your owne parte
least of these my mysfortunes yow beare
the blame ... ffarewell sweet Robyn, if
as I take the, true to me. If not adieu
omnium bipedum nequissimus. Retorne me
thyne answere for my satisfaction, & my
dyamond, & what els thow wilt. The
fornace is prepared wherin our faith
muste be tried. ffarewell till we mete,
which god knowes when.'

When the conspirators were arrested, Poley was committed to the Tower, where his
confession was written. But as Babington
had told him, he was deeply suspected by
the Roman Catholics.

An anonymous informer, writing on
19 September 1586, speaks of 'one Roberte
Poole alias Polley' whom 'the Papists give
out to be the broacher of the last treason'.
They rest persuaded that his committal to
the Tower was a 'blind' after he had revealed the conspirators: he had consorted
with them by the Council's direction.

The Roman Catholic attitude towards him
is more fully set forth in the manuscript
memoirs of the Jesuit, William Weston, preserved at Stonyhurst College. Weston, who
gained notoriety as an exorciser of devils,
was arrested in connexion with the Babington plot on 4 August 1586 and suffered a long
period of captivity.[1]

'Having contrived to insinuate himself
into the intimate acquaintance of the

[1] Quoted by John Morris in *Troubles of our Catholic
Forefathers*, 2nd Series, and by J. H. Pollen, *Mary
Queen of Scots and the Babington Plot*, cxxii–iii. See
also below, pp. 117–20 for Robert Southwell's statements in 1595.

chief Catholics who resided in London he would often receive them in his own house and at a table handsomely supplied. Through this familiarity he gained the reputation of a worthy man, both honourable and devout, and he was often permitted to be present at Mass, the Sacraments and exhortations. He knew exactly how to behave himself, and came to them without a shadow of suspicion.'

Weston goes on to relate how Poley pressed his services upon him:

'His house, his room, his keys, his coffers would all be open to me & might be used by me. Whether he were at home or absent he would make arrangements that in any time of peril or difficulty whatever I should always find a refuge in his house.'

Distrustful of such unreserved offers Weston, according to his own account, gave a cold shoulder to Poley, who revenged himself by betraying him to the Government.

His imprisonment at this time seems to have lasted only six weeks. Among the bills of the Lieutenant of the Tower is one for the expenses connected with the imprisonment of Robert Poley for 18 August 1586 to 'the laste of September the next folowinge beinge syx wicks' amounting in all to vi^{li} xiij^{s}.[1] There is no further similar bill relating to Poley till Christmas Day 1587, and if all the bills have been preserved he would appear to have been at liberty during the fifteen months interval. But he was regarded with suspicion by the Government, as is plain from his protests in a petitioning letter apparently addressed to the Earl of Leicester in which he begs the Earl to employ him in some service at home or abroad. The letter is not dated, but it gives some clues to the time of its composition. It includes the phrases, ' then went your honour immediately to Kylingworth' (Kenilworth) and 'your honour's great business of Parliament'. It must therefore have been written after 29 November 1586, when Leicester returned from the unsuccessful campaign in Flanders, and probably between 15 February and 23 March 1587, when a Parliament was sitting,

---

[1] The details of this and the two other bills mentioned on p. 53 are printed by Miss de Kalb in *The Nineteenth Century and After*, November 1927. They are preserved among the bills of the Lieutenant of the Tower in the Public Record Office, and are numbered E 407/56, Nos. 44, 47, 50.

which the Earl regularly attended. It is remarkable that Poley speaks of having recently introduced to Christopher Blunt a Thomas Audley who had 'married a near kinswoman of your honour's first wife', and who wanted to 'move some suit' to the Earl. What can Leicester have thought of such a reminder of Amy Robsart, if the reference be really to her? Audley had accompanied Poley among other places to Seething Lane, 'where I attended Mr. Thomas Walsingham for my secret recourse to Mr. Secretary, but all to lost labour then and my distress now'. Here again we have direct evidence of Poley's association with Marlowe's patron.

The letter does not seem to have mended Poley's fortunes. At any rate he was again, as has been seen, in the Tower by Christmas 1587 and was there till 25 March 1588. There is no 'bill' extant for the following quarter, but from 24 June till 29 September the Lieutenant of the Tower records the expenses in connexion with his imprisonment as xv^{li} xij^s viij^d. Whether he was free or not during the interval, his confinement cannot have been close for, as before in the Marshalsea, Joan Yeomans was able to visit him, with 'one W. Golder', and to bring him letters from overseas from Christopher Blunt, who was serving in Flanders in 1587-8. Yeomans gives a vivid account in his evidence of how he found his wife reading one of these letters and of her throwing it into the fire.

Ede and Yeomans both confirm the information from the Tower 'bills' that Poley was released about Michaelmas 1588. This was apparently due to the intervention of Sir Francis Walsingham. 'Had not I good lucke to gett owt of the Tower?' Poley asked Yeomans, declaring that 'Mr. Secretarie did deliver him owt'. 'You are greatlie beholdinge vnto Mr. Secretarie', answered Yeomans. 'Naye', said Poley, 'he is more beholdinge vnto me then I am vnto him for there are further matters betwene hym & me then all the world shall knowe of.' He further declared that Walsingham had contracted a disreputable disease in France.

On his release Poley quartered himself on the unfortunate Yeomans, who took Ede 'into his nether room and made very great mone that Poley was come to lodge and did lodge in his house again'. Ede sensibly advised Yeomans to get rid of him, as other-

wise he would 'beguile him either of his wife
or of his life'. And so it proved. On 10
November Poley got Yeomans committed
to the Marshalsea for disregard of a warrant of the Vice-Chamberlain, Sir Thomas
Heneage. Richard Ede again intervened as
a peace-maker, but his efforts, though they
got Yeomans out of prison, ended in failure,
for mistress Yeomans, on pretence that she
was going to market, finally eloped with
Poley.

CHAPTER THREE

Marlowe in London

⁋ The Charges of Kyd and Baines

WHILE Poley was occupied with his nefarious double game of domestic and political intrigue, Marlowe had left Cambridge permanently for London. Though he had held his scholarship for the six years which implied a future clerical career, the growth of his speculative views must have convinced him that he was unfit to take orders. And his temporary Government employment, whatever its nature, may well have helped to turn his attention towards 'civil causes'. The first permanent theatres had recently been established, and he began to write for them.

With his achievement as a playwright and poet, and his place in the history of the English stage, I am not here directly concerned. And regarded merely as documents for his biography the extant earliest editions of the poems and plays are of little avail. Those that bear his name on the title-page are all

posthumous. The two Parts of *Tamburlaine*
were printed by Richard Jones in 1590,
and again in 1592, but neither on the title-
page nor in the entry at Stationers' Hall,
14 August 1590, is the name of the author
given, though we learn that the plays were
acted 'vpon Stages in the Citie of London'
by the Lord Admiral's servants. Marlowe's
authorship rests on the internal evidence
of style, supported by the allusions in Robert
Greene's prefatory epistle to *Perimedes the
Blacksmith* (1588) to 'that Atheist *Tam-
burlan*', followed by a gibe 'at the mad
and scoffing poets, that have propheticall
spirits as bred of *Merlin's* race'. Greene's
attack has also done the service of fixing
the dates of the two Parts as approximately
1587 and 1588. Henslowe's *Diary* records
fifteen performances of Part I and seven
of Part II between 28 August 1594 and
13 November 1595.

The earliest extant edition of *Doctor Faustus*
written by 'Ch. Marlowe' was published
by Thomas Bushell in 1604. Henslowe
records twenty-four performances by the
Lord Admiral's Company between 30 September 1594 and 5 January 159⅞, and
there was a later revival in October 1597.

These do not however help to fix the date of composition which on cumulative, though not conclusive, evidence is generally assumed to be during the winter of 1598-9.

The Jew of Malta was entered to Nicholas Ling and Thomas Millington on 17 May 1594, but was not published as 'written by Christopher Marlo', so far as is known, till 1633, by Nicholas Vavasour, with an epistle dedicatory and prologues and epilogues for the Court and the Cockpit by Thomas Heywood. But an allusion to the death of the Duke of Guise (on 23 December 1588) at the beginning of the play, and Henslowe's mention of a performance on 26 February 159½ give upward and downward limits. 1590 or 1591 is the probable date. Henslowe records thirty-six performances up to 21 June 1596, and some expenses for a revival in or about May 1601.

The Massacre at Paris, ' written by Christopher Marlow ', was published by Edward White in an undated edition, probably not earlier than 1600. Here, as in *The Jew of Malta*, an historical event, the death of Henry III of France, which closes the play, gives an upward limit, 2 August 1589, and Henslowe's first mention of a perform-

ance, a downward limit, 30 January 159⅔.
As Henslowe marks it as a new play, it was
probably composed not long before. It was
acted on this occasion by Lord Strange's
servants. Ten later representations by the
Lord Admiral's Company are recorded between 19 June and 25 September 1594.

Edward II, 'written by Chri. Marlow
Gent.' and acted 'in the honourable citie
of London' by the Earl of Pembroke's servants, was published by William Jones in
1594. It had been registered on 6 July
1593, and there is some reason to think that
Jones issued an edition, no longer extant,
in this year.[1] The performances by the
Earl of Pembroke's company suggest the
winter of 1592–3 as the date of the play.

In the same year as the 1594 edition of
Edward II appeared *Dido, Queen of Car-
thage*, 'played by the Children of her Maies-
ties Chappell' and 'written by Christopher
Marlowe, and Thomas Nash, Gent.' Both
Tanner and Warton in the middle of the

---

[1] Prof. Tucker Brooke in *Mod. Lang. Notes*, May 1909,
gives reasons for the view that a MS. title-page,
dated 1593, and the first seventy lines, containing
variants, inserted in Dyce's copy of the 1598 edition
of the play, are from the 1593 text.

eighteenth century appear to have seen a
poetic elegy on Marlowe's death prefixed
by Nash to this play, but it is not found in
any of the three extant copies. Internal
evidence gives little indication of Nash's
hand in the play and suggests affinities with
both Marlowe's early and later work. The
date, therefore, is uncertain, and the statement of the performance of the play by the
Children of the Chapel does not help. As
Sir Edmund Chambers points out, ' Beyond
its title-page and that of the anonymous
Wars of Cyrus there is nothing to point to
any performances by the Chapel between
1584 and 1600.[1]

The six editions of C[hristopher] M[ar-
lowe's] translation of Ovid's *Amores* (two of
' certaine of Ovid's elegies ' and four of the
' 3 Bookes ') were printed, with Epigrams
by [Sir] J[ohn] D[avies], according to the
title-page ' at Middleburgh ' in Holland.
None of them is dated, but a copy was burned
on 4 June 1599 at Stationers' Hall by order
of the Archbishop of Canterbury and the
Bishop of London. Internal evidence suggests a date of composition during or soon
after Marlowe's Cambridge period,

[1] *The Elizabethan Stage,* vol. iii, p. 426.

' Lucans first booke of the famous Civill warr betwixt Pompey and Caesar Englished by Christopher Marlow ' and ' a booke intituled *Hero and Leander* being an amorous poem devised by Christopher Marlow' were both registered by John Wolf on 28 September 1593. There were, however, transfers of copyright, and the First Book of Lucan, ' translated line for line', was not brought out till 1600 by Thomas Thorpe, with a dedication to Edward Blount, 'in the memory of that pure Elementall wit Chr. Marlow'. Blount himself published in 1598 Marlowe's incompleted part of *Hero and Leander*, with a dedication to Sir Thomas Walsingham, which will be discussed later. In the same year Paul Linley brought out the poem ' finished by George Chapman '.

The net result of what we learn from registration, title-pages, and dedicatory epistles is thus meagre. In themselves they do not indicate that the two Parts of *Tamburlaine*, the only works, so far as we know, printed during his life-time were from his pen: they throw no light on the dates of the composition of his other works. But they give the names of some of the companies who performed his plays, and of Edward Alleyn, on

Heywood's authority, as the actor of the title-part in *The Jew of Malta*. On the performances of the plays Henslowe's *Diary* gives valuable further information, especially for the years immediately after his death.

There is not a single word of personal preface by Marlowe himself, like Shakespeare's dedications of *Venus and Adonis* and *Lucrece* to the Earl of Southampton, or Chapman's of the continuation of *Hero and Leander*, to Lady Audrey Walsingham. And as to Edward Blount's dedication of the unfinished *Hero and Leander* to Lady Audrey's husband, Sir Thomas, this, as will be seen, is a document that conceals much more than it reveals.

One point of interest is to be noted. The dramatist was evidently known among the publishers as 'Marlow', with the variant spellings, Marlo, Marloe, Marlowe. The title-pages and entries at Stationers' Hall show this. But in 1593 he was still, as in his later Cambridge days, 'Marley' to Richard Baines and 'Morley' to the Coroner and his jury. It is therefore to be presumed that the entry in the Middlesex Sessions Rolls, 1 October, 31 Elizabeth (1589), of which the following is an English summary, is concerned with him.

'Richard Kytchine of Clifford's Inne, gentleman, & Humfrey Rowland of East Smithfeilde in the county aforesaid, horner came before me, William Flete-woode, Serjeant at Law and Recorder of the City of London, one of the Justices of our Lady the Queen appointed in the county aforesaid, & became sureties for Christopher Marley of London, gentle-man : to wit, each of the sureties afore-said under the penalty of twenty pounds, and he, the said Christopher Marley, undertook for himself, under penalty of forty pounds . . . on condition that if he the said Christopher shall personally ap-pear at the next Sessions of Newgate to answer everything that may be alleged against him on the part of the Queen, and shall not depart without the permission of the Court.'

If this Christopher Marley is the dramatist, Recorder Fleetwood was occupied during the same year with the affairs of Poley and Marlowe. It was Sidney Lee who first called attention to the importance of the entry (*Athenaeum*, 18 August 1894) when it was printed by J. C. Jeaffreson in vol. 1, p. 189 of the *Middlesex Sessions Roll*. But the problem of the three Christopher Morleys had not then arisen. In any case 'Christopher Marley of London, gentleman' cannot be the seminarist priest, who was only seventeen in 1589. Unless a more likely candidate for jail-delivery of the same name can be found, we may consider that we have to do here with the dramatist.

On a visit to London in 1926, subsequent to the publication of his *Death of Marlowe*, Dr. Hotson made important discoveries about the two sureties.[1] Richard Kytchine of Clifford's Inn is the Richard Kitching who, according to an entry in the *Coram Rege* rolls of the King's Bench, for Hilary Term 1586, acted as attorney for Thomas Meeres of Kent. He is almost certainly to be identified with Richard Kytchyn, who was assessed at five shillings in 1588 on his land in the parish of St. Bartholomew's, Smithfield. He was therefore a man of some property, financially qualified to act as a surety. But his presentment at a later date, 11 April 1594, for a grave felony in this same parish

---

[1] See *Marlowe among the Churchwardens* in *The Atlantic Monthly*, July 1926. The details about Kytchine and Rowland that follow are given in this article.

of St. Bartholomew's, does not say much for
his moral character.

The other surety, Humphrey Rowland, was
taxed eight shillings on goods valued at £3.[1]
He too had a character not above reproach,
for the King's Bench Controlment Rolls for
1586 contain the following entry:

> 'Middlesexia Venire facias octabis Hilarii
> Humfridum Rowland de parochia de Est-
> smythfelde in comitatu Middlesexie yo-
> man responsurum Regine de quibusdam
> transgressionibus et extorcionibus unde in-
> dictatus est per Bagam supradictam.'

What these transgressions and extortions
were we do not know, but from Dr. Hotson's
investigations of the registers of St. Botolph's
Church, East Smithfield, it is evident that
Humphrey Rowland had been a householder
in the parish at least since 1577, with a full
domestic life. On 3 November 1577 'James
Paadge Servaunt vnto Humphrey Rollaund
hornebreaker was Buryed', and on the following 7 December a daughter, Anne, was
also buried. He lost two other children
through the plague at the end of September

[1] In the same East Smithfield Subsidy Roll Jacobus
Morlowe is assessed at 50 shillings on goods value £30.
But there is nothing to connect him with the dramatist.

1582, and in February 1585 his wife, Mary.
On 4 May he was married again, to Eve
Ashe. In the same month he lost his sister,
'Amey Skriwatter wedow', who would
appear to have lived with him. Two sons
of the second marriage died in infancy, in
April 1591 and August 1593. Finally, it
came to light that notwithstanding the transgressions and extortions of 1586 Humphrey
Rowland for six years held the office of
churchwarden.

That a Cambridge graduate who had held
for six years a scholarship intended for
candidates for holy orders should have a
churchwarden among his associates is not in
itself remarkable. But from his arrival in
London Marlowe's notoriety as an 'atheist'
at least equalled his fame as a playwright.
Greene's reference to 'that Atheist Tambur-
lan' in the epistle to the 'gentlemen readers'
of *Perimedes the Blacksmith* (1588) is an
attack on him from both points of view,
and this is elaborated in the dying exhorta-
tion in the *Groatsworth of Wit* (1592) to the
three 'Gentlemen his quondam acquaintance
that spend their wits in making plays'. Marlowe is here 'the famous gracer of Trage-
dians' with whom Greene has said, like the

fool in his heart, 'there is no God'. We would gladly have spared much of Greene's invective for some further details of their 'acquaintance'. The lack of these may, however, be partly due to Henry Chettle who saw the *Groatsworth of Wit* through the press, and who a few months later, in a preface to his own *Kind-Harts Dreame*, stated that he had struck out part of the passage addressed to Marlowe as 'to publish it was intolerable'. Yet Marlowe and Shakespeare, 'the upstart crow . . . in his owne conceyt the only Shake-scene in a countrey', had taken offence. Chettle had then known neither of them, but he had since come into contact with Shakespeare, to whom he makes the most handsome and complimentary amends. In sharp contrast is the avowal that 'with one of them I care not if I never be acquainted', though he reverences his learning. Marlowe was then at the height of his achievement as a dramatist, and had the prestige of the 'learning' of a university graduate. Shakespeare was still more or less in his theatrical apprentice stage and was a poor provincial from Stratford. Yet Chettle, while gratified by his first intercourse with the 'upstart crow', deliberately

held aloof from the dramatist who had fully
arrived.

It is remarkable how little positive evidence
there is of Marlowe's association with other
prominent playwrights. There is nothing
to prove that he and Nash worked together
on *Dido*, though both their names are on
the title-page. Chapman, when he continued
Marlowe's unfinished *Hero and Leander*,
made a vague declaration (Sest. III, l. 159)
of 'how much his late desires I tender'.
But in his dedicatory epistle to Lady Walsingham he says not a word about personal
intercourse with him. Shakespeare quotes
a line from the poem in *As You Like It*,
some seven years after his death, apostro-
phizing him as 'dead Shepherd'. But any
dramatic collaboration between them, if it
took place, has to be inferred purely on internal evidence.

The one certain fact is that Marlowe, as
we know from Thomas Kyd's own statement in his letter to Sir John Puckering
after Marlowe's death on 30 May 1593,
was intimate enough with Kyd for them to
be 'wrytinge in one chamber two yeares
synce', i. e. in the early summer of 1591.
On that occasion some fragments of an here-

tical disputation belonging, as Kyd affirmed, to Marlowe got shuffled among Kyd's papers. When I found these fragments with Kyd's letter (*Harl.* MSS. 6848, ff. 187–9 and 6849, f. 218) in 1898, I thought that they might be from the pen of Francis Kett, the heretical Fellow of Marlowe's college at Cambridge, who was burnt at Norwich early in 1589. But in an article in *Studies in Philology* (April, 1923) Professor W. Dinsmore Briggs has proved that the fragments are part of an anonymous treatise quoted in full for purposes of confutation by John Proctor in 1549 in a book called *The Fal of the Late Arrian*. It is surprising that Marlowe in 1591 should have had in his possession parts of a disputation which had brought its author, as Proctor states, into trouble with the Privy Council in the reign of Henry VIII, and which some forty-five years later was to bring Kyd into suspicion of 'atheism', though the views expressed in it are not atheistic but Socinian.

But whatever the exact brand of Marlowe's heresies may have been, the serious tone of 'the late Arrian's' doctrinal treatise is remarkably different from that of the heterodoxies attributed to the dramatist by a consensus of contemporary witnesses. On the evidence at hand thirty years ago I was inclined to discount their statements, but the newer documents have led me partly to modify my view. Kyd, in the letter first printed by me in 1899, told Puckering that Marlowe's associates were 'Harriot, Warner, Royden, and some stationers in Paules churchyard'. Harriot is the well-known mathematician who had long been in Sir Walter Raleigh's service, and Warner was probably Walter Warner, a mathematical friend of Harriot. Nash has Harriot in mind when he declares in *Pierce Pennilesse*, 'I heare say there be Mathematicians abroad, that will proue men before *Adam*'. It is to Harriot also that the Jesuit pamphleteer, Robert Parsons, referred in his *Responsio ad Elizabethae edictum* (1592), as 'Astronomo quodam necromantico' the preceptor of the 'schola frequens de Atheismo' which Walter Raleigh notoriously held in his house. In the English summary of the *Responsio* the words used are:

> 'Of Sir Walter Rawley's schoole of Atheism by the waye, & of the Conjurer that is M[aster] thereof, and of the diligence vsed to get yong gentlemen of this

Atheism

70

schoole, where in both Moyses, & our Sauior, the olde, and the new Testamente are iested at, and the schollers taughte amonge other thinges, to spell God backwarde.'

It is worth noting that when on Whitsun eve, 2 June 1593,[1] the informer Richard Baines brought charges of blasphemy against 'Christopher Marly' (*Harl.* MSS. 6848, ff. 185–6), he too brings Moses, Harriot, and conjuring into close relation:

'He affirmeth that Moyses was but a

[1] This date rests on the altered heading of the copy of Baines's Note sent to Queen Elizabeth (*Harl.* MSS. 6853, f. 307). The original heading has been scored through and altered to 'A Note deliuered on Whitson eve last of the most horrible blasphemes vtteryd by Cristofer Marly who within iii dayes after came to a soden and fearfull end of his life'. As Whitsun Eve in 1593 was 2 June, and as we now know that Marlowe was killed on 30 May, he did not die three days after the delivery of the Note. If the scribe means this he was mistaken as to the date either of the delivery of the Note or of the dramatist's death. It has been suggested that the meaning is that Marlowe died within three days of uttering the blasphemies. But Baines does not seem to be referring to his utterances on one occasion but to his 'comon speeches'. If he handed in the Note on 2 June, he presumably did not know of Marlowe's death on 30 May.

Iugler and that one Heriots being Sir W. Raleighs man can do more then he.'

I have always—as has been the general attitude of students—heavily discounted Baines's allegations as those probably of a professional spy. But in the light of recent discoveries they cannot be so summarily dismissed as has been customary. Thus as an alternative to the charge of Atheism against Marlowe he brings that of a preference for Papistry:

> 'That if ther be any god or any good Religion then it is the Papistes, because the service of God is performed with more cerimonies, as Elevation of the masse, organs, singing men, shaven crownes, &c. That all protestantes are Hypocriticall asses.'

Without accepting these as Marlowe's *ipsissima verba*, it is evident that Baines's statement must be viewed in a different light now that it does not stand alone, but has to be taken in conjunction with the earlier allegation of 1587 that 'he was determined to have gone beyond the seas to Reames and there to remaine'.

So also with Baines's charge against the

dramatist of treasonable statements and intentions:

> 'That he had as good right to coine as the Queen of Englande, and that he was aquainted with one Poole, a prisoner in newgate, who hath greate skill in mixture of mettalls, and hauing learned some thinges of him, he ment, through help of a cunninge stamp-maker to coin ffrench crownes, pistoletes, and English shillinges.'

As long as Marlowe was thought of merely as a poet and man of the theatre, such charges might be dismissed as idle hearsay. But we now know that he had been mixed up from his Cambridge days with political affairs. Moreover, in another letter in Kyd's hand apparently to Sir John Puckering [*Harl.* MSS. 6848, f. 154], discovered by Mr. Fred K. Brown, and printed in *The Times' Literary Supplement*, 2 June 1921,[1] Kyd makes against Marlowe a specific allegation of disloyalty and intended adhesion to a foreign (as he then was) sovereign:

> 'He wold perswade with men of quallitie

[1] This letter, containing a list of charges against Marlowe, is unsigned, but is in the same hand as the signed letter. *Harl.* 6849, f. 218.

to goe vnto the K[ing] of *Scotts* whether
I heare *Royden* is gon and where if he had
liud he told me when I sawe him last he
meant to be.'

Thus as in 1587 it had been reported that
Marlowe 'was determined to have gone beyond the seas', to remain within an alien
jurisdiction, so in 1593 his talk had given
colour to the belief that he meant to cross
the Border with a similar intention.

And if Kyd thus supports Baines in his
more general allegations of treasonable purposes, the Coroner's inquest puts beyond
doubt his association with 'one Poole', if, as
is the natural inference, he was the Robert
Poole or Poley who was among his companions on the day of his death.

Baines, too, charges Marlowe with being an
active propagandist in daily intercourse of
his 'atheistic' views:

'These things, with many other, shall by
good and honest witnes be aproved to be
his opinions and comon speeches and that
this Marlow doth not only hould them
himself, but almost into every company
he cometh he perswades men to Atheism
willing them not to be afeard of bugbeares
and hobgoblines . . . and almost al men

74

with whome he hath conversed any time will testify the same.'

Kyd in his list of charges makes the same allegation of constant conversational propaganda:

'It was his custom when I knewe him first & as I heare saie he contynewd it in table talk or otherwise to iest at the devine scriptures gybe at praiers, & stryve in argument to frustrate & confute what hath byn spoke or wrytt by prophets & such holie menn . . .

That things esteemed to be donn by devine power might haue aswell been don by observation of men all which he wold so sodenlie take slight occasion to slyp out. . . .'

Both Baines and Kyd give specific instances of Marlowe's sacrilegious jests, and they have a remarkable family likeness. According to the informer, Marlowe affirmed that Moses 'was but a Iugler', and that it was easy for him 'being broght vp in all the artes of the Egiptians, to abuse the Iewes being a rude and grosse people '.

On Kyd's testimony Marlowe applied the same designation to St. Paul:

'That for me to wryte a poem of St.

75

paules conversion, as I was determined, he said wold be as if I shold go wryte a book of fast and loose, esteeming *paul* a Jugler.'

Baines also includes a reference to St. Paul, though in his 'Note' the charge is one of time-serving :

'That all the apostles were fishermen and base fellows, neyther of wit nor worth, that Paull only had witt, but he was a timerous fellow in biddinge men to be subiect to magistrates against his conscience.'

The most realistic touch of all is in a sally put by Kyd into Marlowe's mouth on a less serious theme :

'That the prodigall Childes portion was but fower nobles, he held his purse so neere the bottom in all pictures, and that it either was a iest, or els fowr nobles then was thought a great patrimony, not thinking it a parable.'

Can it be doubted that out of the statements of Baines and Kyd taken together, and supplemented by the less specific allegations of Nash, Parsons, and others, a fairly consistent picture can be framed? Marlowe does not appear as an 'atheist' in the modern sense. Of the workings of the speculative

76

faculty dealing with the fundamental prin-
ciples of religion or of ethics there is little
trace in his reported sayings. We see
instead a rationalist intelligence blasting its
destructive way through all that was held in
reverential awe by its contemporaries and
ruthlessly desecrating the Holy of Holies.
The supernatural is laughed out of court.
'Things esteemed to be donn by devine
power might haue aswell been don by observation of men.' Religion is merely a
matter designed to 'keep men in awe'.
Prophets and apostles are juglers maintain-
ing by their arts an 'everlastinge supersti-
tion' in the hearts of the people. The Scriptures are to be held in no more account
than (to use Nash's parallel) Bevis of Hamp-
ton.

So far we have, in another phrase of Nash,
'the outwarde Atheist' who 'establisheth
reason as his God'. But Marlowe was not a
philosopher conducting an anti-religious campaign by elaborate treatises. His method was
the more formidable one of sap and mine.
Wherever he went, in table-talk and otherwise, he let loose his mordant wit upon sacred
subjects. Banter about the prodigal son's
purse, defamation of the most hallowed

77

Biblical figures, blasphemies now scarcely
printable were mingled together in his 'comon
speeches'. He was a propagandist, provoca-
tive, explosive force. He could not be ignored.
Some, like Kyd, who had been his associates
for a time, ' in hatred of his life & thoughts
. . . left and did refraine his companie'.
Others, like Chettle, openly avowed that
they did not wish to know him. Others,
again, like Baines, petitioned that the mouth
of so dangerous a member should be stopped.

CHAPTER FOUR

The 'Atheism'

of Richard Chomley and Sir Walter Raleigh

BUT there were some who lent a ready ear. One of the allegations by Baines was that one Richard Chomley 'hath confessed that he was perswaded by Marloes reasons to become an Atheist'. Here again Marlowe is brought into relation with government agents of shady character. From 'Remembrraunces of wordes and matter against Richard Cholmeley' (*Harl.* MSS. 6848, f. 190) it is clear that he had been in the service of the Crown, for it is alleged that ' being imployed by some of her Maiesties prevy Counsaile for the apprehenson of Papistes, and other daungerous men, hee vsed, as he saieth, to take money of them and would lett them pass in spighte of the Counsell'. He is probably the Chomley twice mentioned, though unfortunately without his Christian name, in the proceedings of the Privy Council in 1591. On 13 May a war-

rant was issued to John Slater, one of the
Messengers of Her Majesty's Chamber ' to
repair vnto the dwelling places of Mr.
Thomas Drurie,—Roen, one of the Messaun-
gers of her Majesties Chambers, & of Mr. —
Chomley, companions of the said Drurie, or
to anie other place or places whersoever, for
the apprehending and bringing them before
their Lordships without delay, al excuses set
apart, to answeare to such things as shalbe
objected against them '. On 29 July there
was another warrant ' to paie to one Burrage
and Chomeley that apprehended Thomas
Drewry, vi^{li}'. The combination of the names
in the two warrants can scarcely be a mere
coincidence. It looks as if Chomley had
turned against Drury, and helped the Privy
Council to secure his arrest. Then, perhaps
dissatisfied by the reward for this or later
services, he had proved false to his employers.
It is declared that ' he speaketh in generall
all euill of the Counsell; saying that they
are all Athiestes and Machiavillians '.

It may be to these services of Richard
Chomley that his brother Hugh refers in a
letter to Sir Robert Cecil, dated 19 January
159$\frac{1}{2}$, in which he offers to use all his skill
to serve the Queen, and claims that he has

'served faithfully, not seeking to rob his brother of credit, but his brother refused to allow him a partnership. He has been re-conciled twice to his brother Ric[hard] Chomley.[1]

In another document (*Harl.* MSS. 6848, f. 191) a Government informer, who was acting as an *agent-provocateur*, goes into more detail about a treasonable conspiracy that Chomley was organizing:

'Yesterday hee sente two of his companions to mee to knowe if I would ioyne with him in familiaritie, and bee one of their dampnable crue. I sothed the villaynes with faire wordes in their follies because I would thereby dive into the secretes of their develishe hartes, that I mighte the better bewray their purposes to drawe her Maiesties subiectes to bee Athiestes. Their practise is after her Maiesties decease to make a Kinge amonge themselues and liue accordinge to their owne lawes, and this saieth Cholmeley willbee done easely, be-

---

[1] M. Danchin (*Revue-Germanique*, Jan.–Feb., 1914) calls attention to this letter in *Cal. of State Papers* (*Domestic*), Eliz. 1591–4, but it does not prove, as he thinks, that Chomley was in the personal service of Cecil.

cause they bee and shortely wilbe by his and his felowes persuasions as many of their opynion as of any other religion.'

Both these documents are undated, but at the Privy Council held on 19 March 1593 a warrant was issued to George Cobham, one of the Messengers of Her Majesty's Chamber, 'to apprehende Richarde Chomeley and Richarde Stronge and to bringe them before their Lordships'. The Government were warned by their agent that the arrest would be no easy matter. 'This cursed Cholmeley hath 60 of his company and hee is seldome from his felowes and therefore I beeseech your worship haue a special care of your selfe in apprehending him, for they be resolute murderinge myndes.' This may explain the fact that it was more than three months before he was apprehended, and then not by Cobham. On 29 June Justice Young wrote to Sir John Puckering (*Harl.* MSS. 7002, f. 10) to 'advartise' him 'that yestar night, at ix of the cloke, Mr. Wilbrom came to me and brought Richard Chomley with him; he did submet hym selfe to hym'. Young further states that he has committed Chomley to prison, and that 'Chomley sayd vnto my men as he was goyng to preson, that he did

kno the Law, that when it came to pase, he
cold shefte will ynowgh'.

A conspirator who could go to meet his
fate with this grimly humorous gesture
would be a man after Marlowe's heart. But
as M. Danchin has shown, he appears to have
been saved by the intervention of the Earl
of Essex, who on 13 November wrote to Sir E.
Littleton, Sir E. Aston, and R. Bagot, thank-
ing them for their trouble in the matter of
his servant Cholmley, and asking for its con-
tinuance that his innocency may be established.[1] Their efforts must at any rate have
prevented his execution if he was the Richard
Chomley whose name appears (as Danchin
has pointed out) in the Middlesex Session
Rolls, 28 January, 42 Elizabeth.

'True bill that, at Clerkenwell, Co. Mid-
d[lesex] on the night of the said day.
George Collins, yoman, Richard Chomeley gentleman, and William Greene
gentleman, all three late of the aforesaid
parish, broken into the dwelling-house of
Thomas Beddingfielde esq. and stole there-
from an iron chest worth ten shillings and

[1] Historical MSS. Commission, 4th Report, p. 330,
quoted by Danchin, *Rev.-Germanique*, Jan.–Feb. 1914.

a hundred pounds of money in the same chest. Putting themselves " Not Guilty " the three prisoners were remanded.'

And it is through Chomley that we get the only direct contemporary testimony to Marlowe's personal association with Raleigh. Both Kyd and Baines had borne witness to the dramatist's intimacy with Harriot, but to know the 'man' of an Elizabethan nobleman was not necessarily to be familiar with his ' lord '. Kyd had asserted that his own lord could not endure Marlowe's name or sight. But one of the charges against Chomley in ' the Remembrances of words and matter' is that

> ' Hee saieth & verely beleueth that one Marlowe is able to shewe more sounde reasons for Atheisme then any devine in Englande is able to geue to prove devinitie & that Marloe tolde him that hee hath read the Atheist lecture to Sr Walter Raliegh & others.'

This ' lecture' can scarcely have been the treatise part of which was found in Kyd's possession. This was, as we now know, a transcript of a document dating back nearly half a century, and it had not been in Marlowe's hands for about two years. More probably Baines, who appears to have known Chomley, was referring to this 'lecture' when he alleged that Marlowe 'hath quoted a number of contrarieties oute of the Scriptures which he hath given to some great men who in convenient time shalbe named'. Unfortunately for us the 'convenient time' was never to come, and thus Chomley remains our only witness to personal intercourse between Sir Walter and the dramatist. We are not warranted on this slender basis to assume that there was such a familiarity between them as the dedication of *Lucrece* suggests between Southampton and Shakespeare.

In any case when on 'one Wednesdaye sevenight before the Assizes', in the summer of 1593, probably within a month or two after Marlowe's death on 30 May, Sir Walter Raleigh, his half-brother Carew Raleigh, Sir Ralph Horsey, Ralph Ironside, minister of Winterbottom, and others, met at the tables of Sir George Trenchard, at Wolverton, and when towards the end of supper a disputation arose on theological matters, there was no reference to 'the Atheist lecture' or to Marlowe's opinions. The question of what the soul is having been posed by Carew, Sir

Walter asked Ironside to answer it for the benefit of the company :

> ' I have benn (sayeth he) a scholler some tyme in Oxeforde, I have aunswered vnder a Bachelor of Arte & had taulke with diuines, yet heithervnto in this pointe (to witt what the reasonable soule of man is) have I not by anye benne resolued. They tell vs it is *primus motor* the first mover in a man &c.'

Ironside sought to satisfy Raleigh by quoting ' the generall definicion of Anima out of Aristotle 2° de Anima cap: 1°', and thence deducing ' the speciall definicion of the soule reasonable '. But Sir Walter, in this respect no true ' Clerk of Oxenford ', repudiated the Aristotelian definition ' as obscure & intricate '. Similarly, at a later stage of the discussion, he was dissatisfied with the Aristotelian definition of God as ' Ens Entium ', for ' neither coulde I lerne heitherto what god is '.

We have the best warrant for the accuracy of Ironside's account of this ' disputation '. Not only was he giving his testimony on oath before a Commission on Atheism held at Cerne Abbas in March, 1594, but one of the Commissioners, Sir Ralph Horsey, had been among the company at George

Trenchard's table and was thus in a position to check the truth of his story. It was a grave scholastic discussion with nothing of the iconoclastic and ribald elements of the opinions attributed to Marlowe by Kyd and Baines.[1] It is significant of Raleigh's conventional practice, whatever his speculative opinions, that he ended the dialogue by asking 'that grace might be sayed; for that, quoth he, is better then this disputacion'.

In other depositions, however, before the Commission we hear of a member of Sir Walter's 'retinew', Thomas Allen, Lieutenant of Portland Castle, who evidently had something of the mocking humour of Marlowe. Different witnesses declared that 'he is great blasphemer & leight esteemer of Religion; and thereaboutes cometh not to Devine service or sermons'; that he 'did teare twoe Leaves out of a Bible to drye Tobacco on'; that 'when he was like to dye, being perswaded to make himselfe red-

---

[1] The serious character of Raleigh's speculations is shown in his two treatises on *The Soul* and *The Sceptic* (included in vol. viii of the Oxford edition of his works, 1829). Some short extracts from these are quoted by Miss Ellis-Fermor (*Christopher Marlowe*, pp. 163–5).

dye to God for his soule' he answered, ' he woulde carrye his soule vp to the topp of an hill, and runne god, runne devill, fetch it that will have it'.

Harriot's heresies are mentioned by several of the deponents, one of whom ' hath harde that one Herriott attendant on Sir Walter Rawleigh hath been convented before the Lordes of the Counsell for denyinge the re-surrecion of the bodye'. There is no record of such an appearance of Harriot before the Privy Council. Nor, as far as is known, were the examinations at Cerne followed by any action against Raleigh or his friends.

Recent critical speculations, however, has sought to find echoes of the controversies and antagonisms in which Sir Walter was involved in contemporary poetry and drama. Mr. G. B. Harrison has argued on plausible grounds that the heroine of *Willobie his Avisa* (1594) was born at Cerne Abbas, and that she was the hostess of an inn in the neighbouring town of Sherborne, where Raleigh had the lease of the Abbey from January 1592. There is good reason for supposing that both Henry Willobie, the reputed author of the poem, and Hadrian Dorrell, who signs the preface, are fictitious, and that the work is from the pen of Mat- thew Royden, to whose *Astrophell* it has points of close similarity. Royden is mentioned in both Kyd's letters as a friend of Marlowe, and in 1594 Chapman dedicated to him as his 'dear and most worthy friend' his work *The Shadow of the Night*. Royden was therefore more or less closely associated with members of the Raleigh circle, who had their chief rivals in the Essex and Southampton group. Mr. Harrison accepts the probable identification of Avisa's rejected suitor H. W. with Henry Wriothesley, Earl of Southampton, and his friend W. S. with William Shakespeare. Moreover, from the mention of Shakespeare's *Lucrece* in the prefatory verses to *Willobie his Avisa* signed 'Vigilantius: Dormitanus', and the line 'Let *Lucres-Auis* be thy name', Mr. Harrison concludes that the author intended '*Willobie his Avisa* to be coupled in the reader's mind with Shakespeare's *Lucrece* . . . the most important poem produced by the followers of Southampton in 1594'. Whatever may have been Shakespeare's own intention, his readers

'saw in this poem, written for the Essex-Southampton group, a very considerable

likeness between Tarquin the Ravisher
and their enemy, Raleigh the Proud. . . .
And so, in the summer of 1594, the followers of Sir Walter Raleigh, who were
living with him at Sherborne, stung
beyond endurance by these incessant at-
tacks on their patron, composed the poem
of *Willobie his Avisa*, seeking to hold his
enemies up to ridicule, not in any fable
culled from Antiquity, but with the plain
tale of the country hostess who so triumph-
antly humiliated her noble wooers'.

But if the editors of the 'New Cambridge
Shakespeare' be right, an even more important production than either *Lucrece* or
Willobie his Avisa played a part in the war-
fare between the two contending factions.
Love's Labour's Lost, ridiculing the attempt to establish an 'Academie' in de-
fiance of the natural relation of the sexes,
is full of references to blackness and to
night, including the lines (IV. iii. 250-1):

O paradox! Black is the badge of hell
　　The hue of dungeons and the School of
　　　Night.

'The School of Night', the Cambridge
editors urge, is to be identified with Raleigh's

'School of Atheism'. It was, as has been
seen, to Royden, the associate of Marlowe
and of Harriot, that Chapman dedicated his
work *The Shadow of the Night*, which included a *Hymnus in Noctem*. Two lines in
the *Hymnus*:

No pen can anything eternal write
That is not steeped in humour of the Night

find a 'retorting challenge' in Berowne's
cry:

Never durst poet touch a pen to write
Until his ink were temper'd with Love's
     sighs.

Love's Labour's Lost, it is contended, is a
satire upon Raleigh's 'School', and it is
further suggested that it was written in 1593
for a private performance in the house of
some grandee who had opposed Raleigh and
Raleigh's men—possibly the Earl of Southampton's.

These speculations about *Willobie his
Avisa*, *Lucrece*, and *Love's Labour's Lost* are
so interesting and important that reference
has been made to them here. But they do
not directly concern Marlowe, and it is not
necessary to discuss them further. It should
be borne in mind, however, that Kyd in the

summer of 1593 stated his belief that Royden had gone to Scotland ; and that Shakespeare (as the Cambridge editors admit) could
have seen *The Shadow of the Night* only in
manuscript, if *Love's Labour's Lost* was acted
in 1593. The speculations as a whole also
rest upon the assumption of a rather more
intimate relation between the great Elizabethan nobles and their literary adherents
than appears to be fully warranted.

CHAPTER FIVE

Marlowe's Death

and the Coroner's Inquest
Deptford, 30 May to 1 June 1593

IN any case, by the end of May 1593 Marlowe's mouth, to use the phrase of Richard Baines, had been stopped for ever. Kyd had been arrested on or before 12 May, and the fragments of 'the late Arrian's' disputation found in his possession. It was doubtless because of his assertion that these had belonged to Marlowe that on 18 May the Privy Council issued a warrant to Henry Maunder, one of the messengers of Her Majesty's Chamber, 'to repair to the house of Mr. T. Walsingham in Kent, or to anie other place where he shall vnderstand Christopher Marlowe to be remayning, and by virtue hereof to bring him to the Court in his companie, and in case of need to require ayd'.

Thomas Walsingham has already appeared in 1586 in close relations with Robert Poley, and playing a part in the detection of Bab-

ington's plot. He appears to have been engaged in further Government service, under
the direction of his relative, Mr. Secretary.
In November 1589, on the death of his
brother Edmund, he succeeded to the family
estate at Scadbury, Chislehurst. By 1593,
if not earlier, he had in his service Ingram
Frizer. From various legal documents Dr.
Hotson has succeeded in piecing together
considerable information about him. On
9 October 1589 he bought the Angel Inn,
Basingstoke, for £120, but sold it again
within two months. One of the vendors of
the 'Angel' entered at the same time into
an obligation to him for £240, but failed to
discharge the debt, and Frizer obtained
a judgement against him in Easter Term
1592. Here Frizer, styled 'of London,
yeoman' was the complainant, but another
case, in which he was defendant, is more
informative. At a date not earlier than June
1598 Anne Woodleff of Aylesbury, Bucks.,
and her son Drew complained to the Lord
Keeper concerning proceedings of Frizer
'abut fyve years now past'. Drew Woodleff had appealed to Nicholas Skeres for
financial help, and Skeres had in turn ap-
proached Frizer, who promised Drew as-

sistance in return for a signed bond for £60.
But instead of ready money Frizer could
only offer ' a commoditie ' for which Drew
' mighte have threescore pounds (which was
a certayne nomber of gunnes or greate Iron
peeces).' Drew, who must have been a
simpleton, then asked Frizer to sell the
guns on his behalf, and Frizer came back
with ' only Thirtie pounds protestinge that
that was all that he coulde at that tyme
gett ', but ' in truthe the saide peeces or
gunnes were his owne & the xxx^{li} he
broughte his owne and never offered them to
be soulde at all but lett them remayne uppon
Tower Hill '.

Moreover Drew alleged further chicanery.
It was arranged that ' Skeres shoulde con-
trarie to the truthe affirme that he oughte
to the said Fryser xx^{tie} marks in money &
so procure your saide Orator to enter into
Bonde lykewyse . . . to paie vnto him the
saide twentie marks protesting that when he
the saide Fryser should Receive the same
at your Orators hand he would paie it vnto
the saide Skeres '.

This bond was duly sealed and delivered.
Then as Drew had not ' of his and mothers
estate ' enough to make up to the two sums

of £60 and 20 marks he was induced 'in his
then unwarie age' to enter 'into a statute
of cc^li vnto a gentleman of good worshipp
. . . the saide Fryser his then Maister'.

The entry of this 'statute' Dr. Hotson
discovered among the Lord Chamberlain's
papers at the Record Office. On 29 June
1593 'Drew Woodlef of Peterley, Bucks.,
gentleman', was bound to Thomas Walsingham of Chislehurst, Kent, Esquire, in the
sum of £200 to be paid by 25 July 1593.
Thus the gentleman of good worship,
Frizer's master, is proved to be Thomas
Walsingham of Scadbury.

Frizer did not attempt to refute the charges
made by the Woodleffs; he merely pleaded
that they stood outlawed in a plea of debt
in the Court of Common Pleas. The pre-
sumption, therefore, is that the charges
were in substance true. Of his associate
Skeres little is known before the date of
Marlowe's death. Sir Edmund Chambers
has pointed out that in a letter from the Recorder, William Fleetwood, to Lord Burgh-
ley, dated 7 July 1585, 'Nicholas Skeeres'
is mentioned amongst a number of 'maisterles
men & cut-purses, whose practice is to robbe
Gentlemen's chambers and Artificers' shoppes

in and about London'. Except for his share
in the shady transactions with the Woodleffs, there appears to be no further definite
information about Skeres before the day of
Marlowe's death. But on 13 March $159\frac{4}{5}$ he
was arrested by Sir Richard Martin, Alder-
man, 'in a very dangerous company' at the
house of one Williamson. He appears in
the list as 'Nicholas Kyrse, alias Skeers,
servant to the Earl of Essex', and was im-
prisoned in the Counter in Wood Street to
await examination. According to Miss de
Kalb 'there is proof that he was carrying
important post between the Earl and the
Court in 1589, employment for which he
received Government pay'. And she adds
'that there is some reason to suspect that
he was the Earl's man as far back as 1583–4
and acting in special Government service
in conjunction with Marlowe'. It may be
pointed out that in 1583–4, according to
the payments for his scholarship quoted by
Dr. Moore-Smith, 'Marlowe can only have
been absent for a week or so in the first
quarter, perhaps towards Christmas, and for
a fortnight in the Summer'. This would
scarcely give time for 'special Government
service'.

In any case neither Skeres nor Frizer can
have had the varied experience of Robert
Poley, who, together with them, was in
Marlowe's company in the house of Eleanor
Bull, widow, in Deptford Strand, from the
tenth hour before noon on 30 May 1593.
What followed, according to the inquisition
on 1 June, returned by William Danby,
Coroner of the Household, is, since Dr.
Hotson's discoveries, familiar to all:

> 'Prandebant & post prandium ibidem
> quieto modo insimul fuerunt & ambulave-
> runt in gardinum pertinentem domui
> praedicto vsque horam sextam post meri-
> diem eiusdem diei & tunc recesserunt a
> gardino praedicto in cameram praedi-
> ctam & ibidem insimul & pariter cena-
> bant.'

After supper a quarrel arose about the payment of 'le recknynge' between Frizer
and 'Morley'. The latter was lying on
a bed, and the former was sitting near it,
with his back towards it and with the front
part of his body towards the table. Poley
and Skeres were sitting so close to Frizer on
either side of him that he could not take
flight. Whereupon 'Morley' 'ex subito &
ex malicia sua' drew Frizer's dagger, which

Extract from the Register of St. Nicholas Church, Deptford, including among the burial entries for 1592, 'Christopher Marlow slaine by ffrancis ffrezer; the ·1· of June'

he was wearing at his back, and gave him
two wounds in his head, two inches long
and a quarter deep. Frizer, pinned between
Skeres and Poley, 'in sua defensione &
saluacione vite sue', struggled to get back his
own dagger, with which he inflicted on his
assailant

> ' vnam plagam mortalem super dexterum
> oculum suum profundidatis duorum poli-
> cium & latitudinis vnius policis de qua
> quidem plaga mortali praedictus Cristo-
> ferus Morley adtunc & ibidem instanter
> obijt.'

Such was the account that was accepted
by the Coroner's jury of sixteen men who
(as Dr. Hotson has pointed out) were drawn
from various districts. The inquest was
held on 1 June, ' super visum corporis Cris-
toferis Morley ibidem iacentis mortui & in-
terfecti'. The body must have been buried
immediately after the inquest, for the Register of St. Nicholas Church, Deptford, con-
tains the entry under *Anno Dom.* 1593,
' Christopher Marlow, slaine by ffrancis
ffrezer; the ·1· of June'. A fortnight later,
on 15 June, a writ of *certiorari* was issued
to summon the case into Chancery. The
Coroner Danby made his return, and a Par-

don was issued to Frizer on 28 June, on the ground that he slew Christopher Morley 'in defensione ac saluacione vite sue'.

Such, on the face of it, is the plain, unvarnished tale contained in the legal records. Are we justified in going behind them and questioning the truth of the jury's verdict? This has been attacked on various grounds. In the first place the position of the participants in the affray, as described in the Coroner's 'return', has been sharply criticized, particularly by Miss de Kalb (*T.L.S.*, 21 May 1925):

'Marlowe (says the evidence) snatches a dagger from the rear of Friser's belt and deals him two futile flesh-wounds on the head: such insignificant cuts (on the evidence) as might be self-inflicted to corroborate a put-up story; or such as a man, fighting for his life against heavy odds, might get in, slashing wildly, before he was overpowered. But is it conceivable that any man in mortal earnest would recline on a bed to hack at an antagonist who is sitting upright and certain to retaliate? Friser, though seated between Poley and Skeres "so that he could not in any wise get away", is able to grapple with Marlowe, who is behind him on the bed, to struggle with him for the dagger, and to give him a mortal wound—and this without interference from the two other men who (apparently) waited passive. These two inactive observers were exceedingly competent to keep Friser within the reach of Marlowe ; but as for separating them no such reasonable effort is recorded.'

In the same number of *The Times Literary Supplement* Mr. William Poel deals, to the same effect, with a special aspect of the struggle :

'Marlowe could not have inflicted two wounds on Frizer's head "of the length of two inches and of the depth of a quarter of an inch" with either the point or edge of a dagger. Captain Hutton in his book on "Elizabethan Combats" has shown that when quarrels arose it was not unusual for a man to draw his dagger and with the handle pummel the head or shoulders of his adversary in order to hurt him without danger to his life. Frizer's scalp-wounds can only be explained in this way. But the blow that slew Marlowe must have been given with

terrific force by a man intent on killing
his victim, because the blade, where it
was one inch wide, penetrated Marlowe's
brain to a depth of two inches! Yet
Frizer declares that when he gave his
blow he was seated between Skeres and
Poley " and that he could not in any
wise *get away* in his own defence ". But
what his companions had to say on this
matter we are not told, and these men
seem to have been the associates of
Frizer.'

Secondly, there is the suggestion that the
meeting of the quartet at Eleanor Bull's
house was not for social purposes but for
some deeper, and presumably darker, design
which it was to the interest of the survivors
should not be disclosed at the coroner's inquisition.

This point has also been put forcibly by
Miss de Kalb:

' It is legitimate to inquire why Marlowe
(under citation to appear before the Privy
Council) should have met any three men
and spent eight hours or more in retired
colloquy with them, to be slain by one
at the end. We are told that they behaved
themselves decently and " in quiet sort "

—that is, that they were not carousing. But what was their business that required discussion from mid-morning to evening? What had they in common for such long and sober discourse? . . . This death takes place while Marlowe is awaiting cross-examination by his former masters, the Lords of the Privy Council. If there was a deeper cause for quarrelling than the score it is not difficult to come at the nature of it.'

The implication evidently is that Marlowe knew political secrets which his companions were afraid might be disclosed, and that they acted on the maxim, 'Dead men tell no tales'.

Thus we pass to the question of the credibility of the eyewitnesses. Here, again, the question has been incisively raised by Miss de Kalb:

'If Marlowe's death hung in the balance of that day-long conversation, were not these the men to concoct a plausible story? Were they the men to fumble at a little lying? One was a notorious spy; one was an admitted blackguard, useful as a second in any dubious enterprise; the third was a man whose ordinary deal-

ings would not bear inspection, who
played at fraud with the law. Were these
the men to put their necks in jeopardy
by truth-telling? If not, what was their
testimony worth?'

These queries need more discriminating
consideration than they have hitherto received. It would be easier to give convinc-
ing answer if we had the individual depositions as in the examinations before the
Recorder concerning Poley and Mistress
Yeomans. There not only Yeomans and
Ede gave evidence but household servants.
Did the Coroner ask for testimony from
Eleanor Bull or any of the tavern tapsters?
And by which of the principal witnesses were
he and the jury most influenced? Here, I
think, we are now in a position to make
things somewhat clearer than when Dr.
Hotson made his discoveries and when Miss
de Kalb wrote her article.

Frizer appears to have been a man of some
substance, and his shady relations with the
Woodleffs were probably not known at this
time. But he does not seem to have held
any public position before June 1593, and
appearing in the Coroner's Court, with his
unhealed two-day-old wounds, he was vir-

tually himself on trial for murder. Skeres was the *âme damnée* of Frizer, and is usually heard of as a gaol-bird. Poley, as has been seen, had also spent much time in prison, but he was no ordinary rogue. He had been mixed up in great affairs, and had been on familiar terms with political personages and men of high station. He had been in the confidence of Christopher Blunt and the Sidneys; he had talked with Morgan through the windows of the Bastille; he had supped with Anthony Babington before the break-up of the conspiracy; he had (according to his own account) made Mr. Secretary look out of his window and grin like a dog. Such a man would have little difficulty in impressing 'Nicholas Draper, Gentleman, Wolstan Randall, Gentleman, William Curry' and the rest of the sixteen. And we have his own avowal, reported by Yeomans at an earlier date, 'I will sweare and forsweare my selfe rather then I will accuse my selffe to doe me any harme'. It is, I think, a safe inference that (whatever the actual facts may have been) it was mainly the evidence of Poley that got Frizer off and branded Marlowe as the criminal. If the jury knew anything about the playwright's reputation

for 'atheism', and if the Coroner informed
them (as would be natural) that a fortnight
since the Privy Council had ordered his
arrest, their prejudices would be all in Ingram Frizer's favour.

Such are the grounds upon which doubts
may legitimately be raised concerning the
jury's verdict. But are we, therefore, to ac-
cept the conclusion stated somewhat crudely
by Sir George Greenwood in *The Times
Literary Supplement*, 4 June 1925:

> 'The whole story rings false. Friser was
> the murderer and the plea of *se defendendo*
> obviously cannot be sustained. Marlowe
> had evidently been lured into the company
> of three rogues, spies and cut-purses.'

To begin with, the last statement is rhetori-
cally inexact. The three companions of
Marlowe were, in a sense, rogues. But the
word has implications which, as I have said,
do not apply to Poley, and still less was he
a 'cut-purse'. On the other hand, there is
no proof that either Frizer or Skeres was
a spy, or that any of the trio 'lured' Marlowe to his doom. According to William
Vaughan (in *The Golden Grove*, 1600), who,
as will be seen, had evidently good information about the affray, it was Ingram Frizer

106

who had invited Marlowe to a 'feast'. There is nothing that we know to connect him either with Marlowe's employment on Government service during his Cambridge days or with his later 'atheist' propaganda. There is thus no prima facie reason why he should have been determined at all costs to stop Marlowe's mouth for ever. And it is an important point in his favour that, as Dr. Hotson has shown, he retained his connexion to a much later date with the Walsingham family at Scadbury.

On the other hand, the description of Marlowe by Kyd in his letters to Puckering tallies remarkably with the condemnatory phrases in the Coroner's return. 'He was intemperate & of a cruel hart.' 'As I & many others in regard of his other rashnes in attempting soden pryvie iniuries to men did ouerslypp though often reprehend him for it.' Are not these words echoed in 'ira motus versus praefatum Ingramum ffrysar', 'ex subito & ex malicia sua . . . pugionem maliciose adtunc & ibidem evaginabat'? Was not the assault on Frizer, without warning and from behind, the crowning and final instance of Marlowe's 'rashnes in attempting soden pryvie iniuries to men'?

107

There is evidence, too, that the jury did
not perform their duty perfunctorily. They
viewed the body, and took measurements of
the fatal wound over the right eye, as also
of the wounds in Frizer's head. They ascertained the value of the dagger—not a very
relevant detail. They inquired into the proceedings of the whole day—the meeting at
ten o'clock, the dinner, the subsequent quiet
conference and the walk in the garden, and
the supper at six in the afternoon. They
reconstructed in detail the fatal affray that
followed.

Is it legitimate, from the natural desire to
shield the name of a great poetic playwright, and to redress the balance of con-
tempory prejudice against a revolutionary
thinker, on account of some difficulties in
the case, to reverse the verdict in posterity's
court of appeal? I think not. At the most
we may suspend judgement, remembering
that coroners' findings have given cause for
criticism ever since the Elsinore grave-
diggers discussed the rights and wrongs of
Ophelia's Christian burial.

2nd Clown. But is this law?

1st Clown. Ay, marry is't; crowner's-
quest law.

108

CHAPTER SIX

The Survivors

and the Sequel

WE know that the three eye-witnesses of Marlowe's death survived into the next century. It is of Frizer, owing to the researches of Dr. Hotson and Miss de Kalb, that we have the longest record after 1593. He continues to be occupied with legal and financial transactions. In June 1594 he took over from Thomas Smyth a house in the parish of St. Saviour's, Southwark, with possession for three years. But he was driven out by Edmund Ballard, against whom he brought a suit on 17 October for recovery of possession, which was granted to him with £5 damages and 6*d*. costs. The suit against him by the Woodleffs, probably in 1598, has already been described. His master had been knighted in July 1597. It may have been after this that he moved to Eltham, where he appears to have spent the rest of his life. In a deed of sale, discovered by Dr. Hotson, dated in June 1602, he is described as 'late of London, yoman and nowe dwelling at Eltham in the Countye of Kente'. Eltham is near to Chislehurst, and he still kept up his connexion with the Walsingham family. In December 1603, after a delay which required the intervention of Sir John Fortescue, a lease in reversion of some lands belonging to the Duchy of Lancaster, at a rent of £42 6s. 3d., was granted to Ingram Frizer for the benefit of Lady Audrey Walsingham, the wife of Sir Thomas. In 1611 he appears on the Subsidy Roll as one of the two certified assessors of the parish of Eltham, being taxed one and fourpence on a holding of land valued at 20 shillings. Miss de Kalb has further ascertained that he had a daughter, Alice Dixon, and a nephew, John Banckes; that he had sufficient means to keep a maid-servant; that he held a position of respect in Eltham, and was churchwarden from 1605 till his death in August 1627, when he was buried in the church.

He thus died in the odour of sanctity, and evidently 'lived down' any disrepute attaching to his transactions with the Woodleffs or any suspicion of ill-fame as a homicide. The man who killed Marlowe survived long enough to read, if his tastes lay that way, the first Folio of Shakespeare.

Of Skeres little is known after his arrest and imprisonment in the Counter (mentioned above) on 13 March 159⅘. But he seems to have been a regular gaol-bird. On 31 July 1601 the Privy Council issued warrants to the Keeper of the prison of Newgate ' for the removal of Nicholas Skiers and — Farmer, prisoners in his custodie, into Bridewell '. On the information hitherto forthcoming, Skeres was a commonplace miscreant, not a man of some substance like Frizer, nor a resourceful and unscrupulous adventurer in state affairs like Poley.

But before continuing Poley's story it is of interest to note that, according to a discovery of Professor Tucker Brooke,[1] one of Marlowe's sureties in 1589, Richard Kytchyn, was himself guilty on 2 April 1594 of a sudden assault similar to that which began the affray in which the dramatist died. According to the presentment of a London Grand Jury on 11 April, Kytchyn, in the parish of St. Bartholomew the Great, ' leapt upon a certain John Finch of London, gentleman, then &

[1] Quoted by Dr. Hotson in his article, *Marlowe among the Churchwardens*, p. 41.

III

there walking ... and with a dagger of iron &
steel which he had & held in his right hand
he struck, wounded, & maltreated the said
John Fynch so that his life was despaired of.'

Poley's nefarious conduct in the matter of
his elopement with Joan Yeomans does not
seem to have interfered with his employment as a Government agent. There is a
deposition of one Robert Rutkin, broker,
dated probably April 1591, which is obscure
in some of its references, but which shows
that Poley was an agent for the Vice-Chan-
cellor, Sir Thomas Heneage, and that he
was employed on affairs relating to the Low
Countries :

'Robert Rutkin broker saieth that the
party who wrote the lettres vnto him by
the name of Bar[nard] Riche is Michaell
Moody who liveth either at Brussels or
Antwerpe.... The said Rutkin saieth that
his neighbour mencioned in the letter is
one Poolye & that he deliuereth him
letters for Sir Thomas Henneage & sen-
deth letters to him from Sir Thomas
Henneage ... the said Robert Poolye
lyveth in Shorditch.
'He was at the poste this time to loke
for lettres from him but had none & re-

cyueth no lettres from him but that hee
acquanteth Sir Thomas Henneage withall.
Hee was sent over by Sir Thomas Henneage with letters to diuers persons about
a yeare past.'

About a year later Sir Robert Cecil, writing
to Sir Thomas, refers to an interview with
Poley:

'I haue receauyd your lettre & I will
shew it as occasion may serue. I have
spoken with Poly & find him no Foole.
I do suspend all tyll our meeting which
I wish may be shortly.'

According to Miss de Kalb, Poley, on the
very day of Marlowe's death, had in his
charge letters from the Hague to the Court
at Nonesuch. He was a storm-centre in Flanders as elsewhere. Among the depositions
on 7 April 1595 by one Nicholas Williamson, a prisoner in the Gatehouse, is one to the
effect that 'if Pooly or Barnard Maude shall
come againe in to the lowe cuntryes, they are
threatned to be apprehended. Creichton
chargeth Pooley to haue poysoned the Bishop
of Diuelinge (?)'.[1] Here murder is added to

---

[1] The reading is doubtful, but I cannot identify that
name as that of any known Bishopric.

the list of other indictments against Poley,
but so far as I am aware, nothing is known
of the circumstances or the grounds of the
accusation, unless it refers back vaguely to
a suspicion mentioned by J. H. Pollen (*Mary
Queen of Scots and the Babington Plot*, p. ccv)
that in 1585 Poley poisoned in the Tower
Richard Creagh, Archbishop of Armagh.

Before the end of Elizabeth's reign he had
lost his government employment. A long
letter to Sir Robert Cecil dated 17 December
1600 begins, 'Since it pleasde your Honor
to sequester mee from your seruice and
bountye'. He seeks to regain Cecil's favour
by promising to 'search out and discover
the obscure Arte & cunynge which the
Jesuits vse'.

'I find the pollyticke Jesuite to be the
most dangerous personne that anye commonwealth can nourishe or suffer beeing
continvallye whisperinge & busye in sea-
crett & peremptorye oppositions & de-
vices procedinge from theyr proude am-
bityous and violent humors, for the most
parte very dangerous or preiudicyall to
the Prince & State wher they lyve favour'd or forbydden; which maye to the
purpose be fytlyeste examyned and vnder-

stoode by theyr manifoulde procurements and practises againste oure Cuntrye.'

He describes their methods in some detail, and warns Cecil of their hostility to him personally and to the English Queen and State. He then undertakes to provide an effective counterblast to their machinations:

'Howe agreeable & needfull itt is also in some generall volume exactly to examyne aunswer & controule [i.e. contradict] the particular abuses of their sedicyous and pestilent Bookes, I humblye refer to your honorable Consyderation: confidentlye assuringe you that if it shall please your Honor to accepte the offer & give supportaunce & means needfull to the performance of so importante a businesse as this discoverye wyll bee: that then with learninge & knowledge sufficyent a Booke shal be wrytten & sett forthe, much more substancyall to the effects afore specyfyde then any hath beene heretofore publishde in that kinde.'

Poley sent with his letter an example, from an eminent pen, of the type of literature that he was eager to expose and confute:

'The Booke inclosde was (as I thinke

your Honor knowes) 5 years since dis-
perste in wrytten Coppyes by the Author
R. Suthwell. And lately by Garrett, Garnett and Blackwell putt in printe though
foreadvisde by good discretion nott to do
itt. Wher the leafe is putt in your
Honour maye readylye finde howe they
deale with Sir Fra[ncis] Walsingham, I
proteste most falcelye slandringe him and
wyckedlye abusing him.'

The book was evidently the pamphlet by
Robert Southwell, the Jesuit poet and con-
troversialist, entitled *An Humble Supplication to Her Maiestie.* It was printed anony-
mously, and is dated at the end 14 December
1595 as well as 1595 on the title-page.[1]
It is an eloquent, uncompromising *apologia*
for the Jesuits as propagandists of what in
Southwell's eyes is the only saving faith:

' The whole and onely intent of our comminge into this Realme is no other, but
to labour for the saluation of soules, and
in peaceable and quiet sort to confirm
them in the ancient Catholike faith, in
the which theyr forefathers liued & died,

[1] The copy in the British Museum, one of the very
few extant, has a large number of MS. corrections in
a contemporary hand.

these thousand foure hundred yeares, out
of which we undoubtedly beleeue it is im-
possible that any soule should be saved.'

Poley probably chose this particular work
to send to Cecil because in the attack upon
the memory of Sir Francis Walsingham
Southwell magnified the part played by
Poley himself in the Babington plot. He
states in its most explicit and extreme form
the contemporary Roman Catholic thesis
that Babington and his accomplices were
dupes drawn into a net by Poley as the
chief *agent-provocateur*. Cecil was the last
man to believe this, but it might help to
impress him with a sense of Poley's importance.

'As for the action of *Babington*, that was
[in truthe]¹ rather a snare to intrap them,
then any deuise of their owne, sith it
was both plotted, furthered, & finished,
by S[ir] *Frauncis Walsingham*, & his
other complices, who laied & hatched al
the particulers thereof, as they thought
it wold best fall out to the discredit of
Catholiks, & cutting of the Queene of
Scots; for first it is to be known to all,

¹ Added in MS.

that *Poolie* being Sir *F. Walsinghams*
man, and throughly seasoned to his Mais-
ters tooth, was the chiefe instrument to
contriue & prosecute the matter, to draw
into the net such greene wittes, as (fearing
the generall oppression, and partly angled
with golden hookes) might easilie be ouer
wrought by M. Secr. subtile & sifting wit:
for *Poolie* masking his secret intentions vnder the face of Religion, and abusing with
irreligious Hypocrisie all Rites & Sacraments to borrow the false opinion of a
Catholike, still feeding the poore gentlemen with his masters baits, and he holding
the line in his hand, suffered them like
silly fishes to play themselues vppon the
hooke, till they were throughly fastened,
that then he might strike at his own
pleasure, and be sure to drawe them to a
certaine destruction. And though none
were so deepe in the very bottome of
that conspiracy as *Poolie* himselfe, yet
was hee not so much as indited of any
crime, but after a little large imprisonment (more for pollicy then for any
punishment) set at liberty, & is more
credit then euer he was before: for it
being a set match & he hauing so well

performed his euil part (though to please *Babes*) A stroke was given to beat him, yet doubtlesse he was largely fed in priuie pay, as so Christian pollicy did best deserue.'

Southwell was right, as has been seen, in stating that Poley had only a 'little large imprisonment' immediately after the Babington conspiracy. But he was mistaken in his view that Poley was in greater credit than before with Elizabeth's advisers. His letter to Leicester and his imprisonment in 1587–8 disprove this, though he was again employed later on government service. Southwell's crowning indictment is contained in the following passage:

'It is further knowen that the coppie of that letter which *Babbington* sent to the Queene of Scots, was brought ready penned by *Poolie*, from M. Secretary: the answere whereof, was the principal grounds of the Queenes condemnation. There was also found in Sir *Fraucis Walsinghams* accountes after his decease, a note of 7000 pounds bestowed vpon [*Nawe*][1] & *Curlie*, who being the Queenes Secretaries, framed

---

[1] Substituted in MS. for the printed *Nato*.

such an answere as might best serue for a bloody time, & fit his intention that rewarded them with so liberall a fee.'

It may reasonably be conjectured that it was here that Poley put in a leaf to draw Cecil's special attention. For Southwell here asserts that Babington's letter of 12 July 1586 to Mary Queen of Scots, in which he offered to murder Elizabeth, was composed by Sir Francis Walsingham and brought to Babington 'ready penned' by Poley; and that Mary's answer on 17 July, agreeing to the proposal, was the work of her secretaries influenced by an enormous bribe.

It is sufficient to say that the authenticity of both Babington's and Mary's letters has been overwhelmingly demonstrated for all who do not follow in the tradition of Southwell's partisanship. But what I am more concerned with here is the curiously similar and sinister association of Poley with the tragedies of the Queen of Scots on the one hand and of Marlowe on the other. The partisans of Mary in the sixteenth century accused Poley of being privy to the fabrication of a letter, which led up to what they considered the political murder at Fotheringay. The partisans of Marlowe in the twentieth cen-

tury, who dispute the verdict at the inquest,
implicate Poley in the fabrication of evidence to conceal what was presumably a political murder at Deptford. Poley has certainly no character to lose, but I submit that in both these cases the accusation is groundless.

His letter to Cecil of 17 December 1600 is apparently the last memorial of him in the Public Record Office. But the Hatfield MSS. give us final glimpses of him during another year and a half.[1] In July 1601 he tries to smuggle into England a young cousin, George Cotton, who had been for two years a student at St. Omers, but who was stopped at Dover by the Warden of the Cinque Ports. On 18 July 1602 he again writes to Cecil about the Jesuits, sending him information derived from Robert Barrois, a priest. He avers that Cecil's low estimate of his previous services 'is the cause that I haue not since presented myself with offer of my duty, although I much desire my endeavours might please you, my necessities needing your favour'.

---

[1] References to these are given by Sir Edmund Chambers in a review of Dr. Hotson's *The Death of Christopher Marlowe* (*Mod. Lang. Rev*, January 1926). His quotations are from Hatfield MSS. xi. 216, 278, 302, and xii. 230.

So in the ebb-tide of his fortunes he disappears from view. But whatever were his crimes and follies, the adventurer was born under no ordinary star who crossed the paths of Christopher Blunt and Anthony Babington, of Francis and Thomas Walsingham, of Philip and Frances Sidney, of Mary Stuart and Christopher Marlowe. He is the very genius of the Elizabethan underworld.

There is thus evidence that the three companions of Marlowe on the day of his death survived into the next century, and one of them at least into the reign of Charles I. The circumstances of the affair, in the official version, must have been known to a considerable body of people—the Coroner and the sixteen jurymen, the officials of the Court of Chancery through whose hands the legal documents concerning the inquest and the pardon passed, the households of Eleanor Bull and the Walsinghams. It is therefore surprising that the references to the event in the years immediately following should be so comparatively scanty and so curiously vague or misleading. Mistakes begin on the very day of the inquest when the entry of his burial in the St. Nicholas Church Register gives the Christian name of 'ffrezer' as 'ffrancis' instead of Ingram. Nor is there any indication in the churchyard of the place of the grave.

There are two copies of Richard Baines's Note concerning Marlowe's blasphemies. One of these (*Harl.* MS. 6848, ff. 185–6) is the original document; the other is the replica sent to the Queen. In the latter, as has been mentioned above, the original title is scored through and altered to 'A Note deliuered on Whitson eve last of the most horrible blasphemes vtteryd by Cristofer Marly who within iii days after came to a soden & fearfull end of his life'. Apart from the difficulty of dates already discussed, the official scribe here is tantalizingly vague; his phrase would cover any form of accidental death.

Thomas Kyd's letters to Sir John Puckering were written after (probably soon after) Marlowe had met his fate, for he says, 'It is not to be nombred amongst the best conditions of men, to taxe or to opbraide the deade'. Kyd paints Marlowe in the darkest colours, but he gives no hint that he had brought on his own doom by an unprovoked assault, though, as has been seen, the words 'his other rashnes in attempting soden pryvie iniuries to men' might well cover the Dept-

123

ford stabbing affair. Another contemporary playwright and poet, George Peele, uses common form when in the *Prologue to the Honours of the Garter*, published in 1593, he apostrophizes 'Marley' as 'unhappy in thine end'.

And strangest of all, the only contemporary who appears to allude in the same year with any particularity to the playwright's death is completely misleading. Gabriel Harvey had come up to London in August 1592 to attend to legal affairs concerning the estate of his brother John who had died in July. He stayed in London, apparently at the house of his printer John Wolf in St. Paul's Churchyard till towards the end of July 1593. Marlowe's tragic fate must have caused consternation in 'Paul's', where, as Kyd tells us, he had friends. Moreover, another brother of Gabriel Harvey, Richard, had been Rector of Chislehurst since 1586 [1] and therefore in touch with the Walsingham household. Gabriel Harvey was thus in

---

[1] He had been collated on 1 October 1586, and again on 6 December. He was licensed to preach on 18 September 1587. Marlowe would appear to have heard him on a visit to Scadbury, for he is reported to have called him an ass, fit to preach about nothing but the iron age.

a position to get accurate information from more than one source. Yet, to all appearance, he labours, for edifying purposes, the circumstance that Marlowe died of the Plague, which was rife in 1593! A poetical epilogue to *A New Letter of Notable Contents*, addressed to Wolfe and dated from Saffron Walden, 18 September 1593, begins with a sonnet on '*Gorgon*, or the Wonderfull yeare'. This records leading events of 'the fatall yeare of yeares...Ninety Three', and ends the recital with 'Weepe Powles, thy *Tamberlaine* voutsafes to dye'. The Tamberlaine of 'Powles' who died in 1593 must be Marlowe. What then is to be made of the last section of the Epilogue, the 'Glosse'?

Is it a Dreame? or is the *Highest minde*
That euer haunted Powles or hunted winde,
Bereaft of that same sky-surmounting breath,
That breath that taught the Tempany to
    swell.
He & the *Plague* contended for the game.
The hawty man extolles his hideous
    thoughtes,
And gloriously insultes upon poore soules,
That plague themsealves: *for faint harts
    plague themselves*

.   .   .   .   .

The graund Dissease disdain'd his toade
    Conceit
And smiling at his tamberlaine contempt,
Sternely struck-home the peremptory
    stroke,
He that nor feared God, nor dreaded Diu'll,
Nor ought admired but his wondrous
    selfe . . .
Alas! but Babell Pride must kisse the pitt.

It might be possible to wrest some other
meaning out of part of this, but 'The graund
Dissease . . . sternely struck-home the peremptory stroke' must surely imply Marlowe's death from the plague. Yet the real
fact of his instantaneous death-wound from
Frizer's dagger would have been far more
impressive, as a moral warning, than his
demise from the pestilence that carried off
its thousands without discrimination. The
more Harvey's references are considered the
more enigmatic they become.[1]

Not so with the next known account of
the event, by Thomas Beard, in his *Theatre*

---

[1] Dr. Hale Moore in an article on *Gabriel Harvey's
References to Marlowe* (*Studies in Philology*, July, 1926)
throws light on incidental points, but does not help
to solve the basic problem.

of Gods Judgements, chap. 25 (1597). The work is a translation from the French, illustrating 'the admirable Iudgements of God upon the transgressours of his commandements'. Among the three hundred additional examples with which Beard augmented his version was the divine punishment of 'one of our own nation, of fresh and late memory, called *Marlin*', of whose atheism he gives the conventional account, and then continues:

> 'It so fell out that in London streets as he purposed to stab one whome hee ought a grudge vnto with his dagger, the other party perceiuing so auoided the stroke, that withall catching hold of his wrest, he stabbed his owne dagger into his owne head, in such sort, that notwithstanding all the meanes of surgerie that could be wrought, hee shortly after died thereof.... But herein did the iustice of God most notably appeare, in that he compelled his owne hand which had written those blasphemies to be the instrument to punish him, and that in his braine, which had deuised the same.'

This is, at any rate, an effective piece of 'tendencious' narrative. It was necessary

for Beard's purpose that Marlowe's own hand
should be the instrument of his death, without it being a case of suicide. And though he
thus gives a twist to the facts he knew not
only that Marlowe was killed in a brawl,
but that the two combatants made use of the
same dagger—a very unusual circumstance.
And if Dr. Hotson is right in his ingenious
conjecture that 'London streets' is a printer's error for 'London streete', a thorough-
fare in East Greenwich (Deptford being West
Greenwich), Beard got within 'a few hundred yards' of the actual scene of Marlowe's
death.

But in the next year, 1598, Francis Meres
in his *Palladis Tamia* supplemented Beard's
account, to which he refers his readers, with
highly coloured details:

> 'As the poet *Lycophron* was shot to death
> by a certain riual of his: so *Christopher
> Marlow* was stabd to death by a bawdy
> seruing man, a riuall of his in his lewde
> love.'

Here Meres's obsession with parallels, which
dominates his tractate, works more mischief
than Beard's theological fanaticism. Frizer,
though in the service of Thomas Walsingham, was not a 'seruing man', and 'le

recknynge', not 'lewde love', was the cause
of the affray. The further flourishes that
Anthony Wood and later writers have added
to the rodomontade of Meres are well known.
But in 1600 William Vaughan, drawing evidently upon independent information, gave
in his *Golden Grove* an account that in many
respects hit the mark:

> 'It so hapned that at Detford, a little
> village about three miles distant from
> London, as he meant to stab with his pon-
> yard one named Ingram, that had inuited
> him thither to a feast, and was then playing
> at tables, he quickly perceyuing it, so
> auoyded the thrust, that withall drawing
> out his dagger for his defence hee stabd
> this Marlow into the eye, in such sort,
> that his braines comming out at the dag-
> gers point, hee shortlie after dyed.'

Vaughan, of course, goes wrong in stating
that two weapons were used, but this proves
that his account is not based upon the Coroner's inquisition, and that it therefore has
independent value. Hence it is important
that he should be right about the place of
the affray and the identity of Marlowe's
slayer—whom he calls, after a fashion of the
time, by his Christian name only. The two

details that Ingram Frizer was the host at the entertainment, and that he was playing at tables [i.e. backgammon] are not inconsistent with the legal record, and may be correct. At any rate there was no need to insert them to point the moral, which Vaughan, like Beard, was anxious to enforce: 'Thus did God, the true executioner of diuine iustice, worke the ende of impious Atheists'.

But those who were making theological capital out of the playwright's death did not have it all their own way. In 1598 Edward Blount brought out an edition of Marlowe's unfinished poem, *Hero and Leander*. In the light of the facts, as we now know them, of the fatal affray on 30 May 1593, his dedication of the work to Sir Thomas Walsingham is a remarkable document:

'Sir, wee thinke not our selues discharged of the dutie wee owe to our friend, when wee haue brought the breathlesse bodie to the earth: for albeit the eye there taketh his euer farwell of that beloued obiect, yet the impression of the man, that hath beene deare vnto us, liuing an after life in our memory, there putteth vs in mind of farther obsequies due vnto the

130

deceased. And namely [i.e. especially] of the performance of whatsoeuer we may iudge shal make to his liuing credit, and to the effecting of his determinations preuented by the stroke of death. By these meditations (as by an intellectual will) I suppose my selfe executor to the vnhappily deceased author of this Poem, vpon whom knowing that in his life time you bestowed many kind fauors, entertaining the parts of reckoning and woorth which you found in him, with good countenance and liberall affection: I cannot but see so far into the will of him dead, that whatsoeuer issue of his brain should chance to come abroad, that the first breath it should take might be the gentle aire of your liking: for since his selfe had been accustomed thervnto, it would prooue more agreeable & thriuing to his right children, than any other foster countenance whatsoeuer.'

Who would dream that behind the bland and unctuous phrases of this dedication there lay the story of Marlowe's sudden blow from behind at Frizer, the fatal affray and the viewing of 'the breathlesse bodie' by the Coroner's jury before it was 'brought to

the earth'? And what did Sir Thomas
Walsingham, with whose family Frizer retained his connexion for at least ten years
after the Deptford homicide, think of such
expressions as the 'vnhappily deceased author of this Poem' and 'the effecting of his
determinations preuented by the stroke of
death'? To one who had had first-hand information about the tragedy of 30 May
1593 these conventional flourishes must
have sounded strangely unreal. Had Blount
in view not so much Sir Thomas as the
general reading public, and is this indirect
apologia a counterblast to the fulminations
of Beard and Meres?

There is no need to assume, as has been
done, that Blount's 'impression of the man,
that hath beene deare vnto us, living an after
life in our memory' was shared by Shakespeare in his invocation, through the lips of
Phebe (*As You Like It*, III. v. 80–1), of the
poet from whose *Hero and Leander* he quotes
approvingly a pregnant line :

Dead Shepherd, now I find thy saw of might:
'Who ever lov'd, that lov'd not at first sight?'

But it is to say the least, a remarkable coincidence, that in the same Act of the same
play (III. iii. 9 ff.) Touchstone should use

132

enigmatic words to which the statement about 'le recknynge' in the Coroner's inquisition gives for the first time a possible clue :

> 'When a man's verses cannot be understood nor a man's good wit seconded with the forward child Understanding, it strikes a man more dead than a great reckoning in a little room.'[1]

The parallel here may be merely fortuitous. In any case the echoes of the tragedy, within the lifetime of the survivors, are, as has been seen, so divergent that the lesson of caution in taking at its face value even contemporary evidence is driven home anew.

But whatever be the truth about the details, even about the main circumstances, of the

[1] Since Mr. Oliver F. W. Lodge first suggested that Shakespeare was here referring to Marlowe's death (in *T. L. S.*, 14 May 1925) he has been supported by Mr. W. Poel, *T. L. S.*, 21 May, Mr. Paul Reyher, 9 July 1925, and by Professor Dover Wilson in the 'New Cambridge' edition of *As You Like It* (1926). The reviewer of this edition in *T. L. S.*, 30 December 1926, maintained that this imputed 'brutality of sentiment' to Shakespeare 'who could joke in public on the sordid tragedy of the greatest of his fellow poets'. In *T. L. S.*, 6 January 1927, Professor Wilson and Mr. Lodge disavow this imputation.

affray in which Marlowe met his death, one thing is abundantly clear. No one can hope to understand the Elizabethans who does not realize that they 'lived dangerously'. To test them by modern standards of morality or maxims of worldly prudence is to go astray. Men who were constantly face to face with violent revolutions of fortune, who were surrounded by a network of espionage and intrigue, whose words or actions might bring them at any moment to the Tower or Newgate, to the block or the stake, were not predestined to be patterns of scrupulous rectitude. Not only men of the underworld like Poley, Chomley, and Frizer, but statesmen and persons of quality, Christopher Blunt, Francis Walsingham, Walter Raleigh, are far from conforming with the codes that would be binding on them to-day. Even a Philip Sidney in *Astrophel and Stella* gives voice to his passion, idealized and transfigured though it be, for the woman who had become the wife of a rival. And as to the writer of the greatest of all Elizabethan sonnet-series, can we really credit the suggestion that Shakespeare 'probably returned to his native town and home every summer or autumn for months at a time, and there prepared for the coming Christmas season, writing happily and swiftly in the midst of his family and friends'?[1] The triangular drama of the poet, the noble patron, and the dark lady comes between us and this rose-coloured idyll of domestic bliss.

And what finally of Christopher Marlowe? There is perhaps no figure among the great Elizabethans whom it is so difficult to approach without a sympathetic bias. He comes trailing the clouds of glory of the pioneer, of the herald of the full dramatic day. His is the magnetic appeal of genius cut down in its prime, with rich achievement, and with an even richer promise unfulfilled. But it is not only as playwright and poet that he wins the suffrages of to-day. He challenged with uncompromising boldness the religious and political orthodoxies of his time, and thus is secure of the sympathies of every generation, and not least our own, that seeks to reconstruct the bases of its intellectual and social life. Hence there has been a natural tendency for his lovers and admirers (among whom I am not the least ardent) to become

---

[1] From the Preface to E. I. Fripp's *Master Richard Quyny*. My scepticism does not imply any lack of appreciation of an otherwise valuable volume.

partisans, to look upon every charge brought against him by his contemporaries as the invention of jealousy, malice, or constituted authority on its defence against a dangerous rebel. Thus the witness of Greene, of Baines, of Kyd, not to speak of Beard and Vaughan, has in turn been looked upon as suspect. Even when the dry unimpassioned formulae of the Coroner's inquisition were brought to light recording that Ingram Frizer slew Christopher Marlowe 'in defensione ac saluacione vite sue', a hue and cry was at once started against the acceptance of the verdict.

The attempt has therefore been made in these pages to reconsider the evidence as a whole, and to weigh it in the balance. There is much that we have to discount— the professional rivalry of fellow dramatists, the anxiety of Kyd to clear himself of the suspicion of 'atheism', and the desire of Baines to secure an informer's reward. Above all we have to remember that Poley's was the voice that would carry most weight with the Coroner's jury, and that he was a past master in all the arts of equivocation. But when all this has been allowed, the fact remains that the evidence from the various sources is consistent, and that it presents a figure of passionate impulse and restless intellect, quick at word and blow, equally ready with the dagger-point and the no less piercing edge of a ruthless dialectic. The combination in Christopher Marlowe of such characteristics with the dramatic and lyrical genius that created *Tamburlaine* and *Dr. Faustus*, *Edward II* and *Hero and Leander*, is one of the marvels of the English Renaissance. In Florence or in Venice he would have breathed congenial air. It was Fortune's crowning irony that this most Italianate of Elizabethan Englishmen should have been born and fostered under the shadow of the central sanctuary of the *Ecclesia Anglicana*.

APPENDIX ONE

ALLEGATIONS AGAINST MAR-LOWE IN THOMAS KYD'S LETTERS

A

Part of a letter signed 'Th[omas] Kydd' to Sir John Puckering, the Lord Keeper, in which Kyd defends himself from the charge of Atheism (Harl. MSS. 6849, f. 218).

B

A letter in the same handwriting as *A*, apparently also addressed to the Lord Keeper (Harl. MSS. 6848, f. 154). If there was a signature as far below the body of the letter as in *A*, it may have been cut away.

In the following transcript the abbreviations in both letters have been expanded.

A

When I was first suspected for that Libell that concernd the state, amongst those waste & idle papers (which I carde not for) & which vnaskt I did deliuer vp, were founde some fragmentes of a disputation, toching that opinion, affirmd by Marlowe to be his, and shufled with some of myne (vnknown to me) by some occasion of our wrytinge in one chamber twoe yeares synce.

My first acquaintance with this Marlowe, rose vpon his bearing name to serve my Lord although his Lordship never knewe his service, but in writing for his plaiers, ffor never cold my Lord endure his name or sight, when he had heard of his conditions, nor wold indeed the forme of devyne praiers vsed duelie in his Lordships house, haue quadred with such reprobates.

That I shold loue or be familer frend, with one so irreligious, were verie rare, when *Tullie* saith *Digni sunt amicitia quibus in ipsis inest causa cur diligantur* which neither was in him, for person, quallities, or honestie, besides he was intemperate & of a cruel hart, the verie contraries to which, my greatest enemies will saie by me.

It is not to be nombred amongst the best conditions of men, to taxe or to opbraide the dead *Quia mortui non mordent.* But thus muche haue I (with your Lordships favor) dared in the greatest cause, which is to cleere my self of being thought an *Atheist*; which some will sweare he was.

ffor more assurance that I was not of that vile opinion, Lett it but please your Lordship to enquire of such as he conversd withall, that is (as I am geven to vnderstand) with *Harriot*, *Warner*, *Royden* and some stationers in Paules churchyard, whom I in no sort can accuse nor will excuse by reson of his companie; of whose

consent if I had been, no question but I also
shold haue been of their consort, for *ex minimo
vestigio artifex agnoscit artificem.*

B

Pleaseth it your honorable lordship toching
marlowes monstruous opinions as I cannot but
with an agreved conscience think on him or
them so can I but particulariz fewe in the respect
of them that kept him greater company. How-
beit in discharg of dutie both towardes god
your lordships & the world thus much haue I
thought good breiflie to discover in all humble-
nes.

ffirst it was his custom when I knewe him
first & as I heare saie he contynewd it in table
talk or otherwise to iest at the devine scriptures
gybe at praiers, & stryve in argument to frustrate & confute what hath byn spoke or wrytt
by prophets & such holie menn.

1. He wold report St John to be our savior
Christes *Alexis* I cover it with reverence and
trembling that is that Christ did loue him with
an extraordinary loue.

2. That for me to wryte a poem of St *paules*
conversion as I was determined he said wold
be as if I shold go wryte a book of fast & loose,
esteeming *Paul* a Jugler.

3. That the prodigall Childes portion was but
fower nobles, he held his purse so neere the
bottom in all pictures, and that it either was a

iest or els fowr nobles then was thought a great
patrimony not thinking it a parable.

4. That things esteemed to be donn by devine
power might haue aswell been don by observation of men all which he wold so sodenlie take
slight occasion to slyp out as I & many others
in regard of his other rashnes in attempting
soden pryvie iniuries to men did ouerslypp
thogh often reprehend him for it & for which
god is my witnes aswell by my lordes comaund-
ment as in hatred of his life & thoughts I left
& did refraine his companie.

He wold perswade with men of quallitie to goe
vnto the k[ing] of *Scotts* whether I heare *Royden*
is gon and where if he had liud he told me when
I sawe him last he meant to be.

APPENDIX TWO

A LIST OF PRINCIPAL DOCUMENTS

Chapter I. *Canterbury and Cambridge. The Three Christopher Morleys*

1. The Register Booke of the Parish of St. George the Martyr within the Citie of Canterburie.

    [Printed from the original Registers by J. M. Cowper, 1891. Facsimile of the entry of Marlowe's baptism in J. H. Ingram's *Christopher Marlowe and his Associates* (1904).]

2. MS. Accounts of the King's School, Canterbury, in the Cathedral Library.

    [Facsimile of Treasurer's accounts of payments made in 1578–9 to King's School Scholars, including Marlowe, in Ingram, *op. cit.*]

3. MS. Cambridge Matriculation Lists in University Registry.

4. MS. Grace Books of the University of Cambridge.

    [Facsimiles of entries of Marlowe's admission to B.A. and M.A. degrees in Ingram, *op. cit.*]

5. MS. Corpus Christi College Admission Book (Registrum Parvum).

    [Facsimile of entry of Marlowe's admission among the Pensioners, in Ingram, *op. cit.*]

6. MS. Corpus Christi College Order Book.

7. MS. Corpus Christi College Accounts (Audits, &c., 1575–90).

> [Extracts relating to payments of Marlowe's scholarship 1580–5 and 1586–7, given by G. C. Moore Smith in 'Marlowe at Cambridge' (*Modern Language Review*, January, 1909).]

8. The Privy Council MS. Register, 29 June 1587. Entry 'Whereas as it was reported that Christopher Morley', &c.

> [Printed in *Acts of the Privy Council*, ed. Dasent, vol. xv, pp. 140–1, and in J. Leslie Hotson's *The Death of Christopher Marlowe* (1925), pp. 58–9, as 'A Certificate from the Privy Council in favour of Marlowe'.]

9. Historical MSS. Comm., Salisbury MSS., xii. 211–12. Letter from William Vaughan from Pisa, 14 July 1602, to Privy Council concerning 'one Christopher Marlow'.

> [Reprinted in Hotson, *op. cit.*, pp. 60–1.]

10. MS. Bills of Keepers of the Gatehouse Prison, Westminster, 1596–1606. Entry in sheet from 25 June to 23 September 1604 *re* 'Christopher Marlowe *alias* Mathews, a seminary preist'.

> [Quoted by Sir Israel Gollancz in a letter to *The Times*, 23 June 1925, on 'The Other Marlowe'.]

11. MS. Records of the English College at Valladolid. Entries *re* John Matthew (Mathews) *alias* Christopher Marler, 1599–1603.

> [Quoted by J. B. Whitmore in a letter to *The Times*, 24 July 1925, on 'The Other Marlowe : Fresh Evidence for Identity'. See also further letter from Sir I. Gollancz on 'The Other Marlowe' in *The Times*, 25 July 1925.]

12. Calendar of State Papers relating to English Affairs, preserved principally at Rome, vol. ii, 1572–8, ed. J. M. Rigg (1926).

> [Letters from the Nuncio in Paris to the Papal Secretary of State, 23 and 26 June 1578, *re* Alfonso Ferrabosco.]

Chapter II.   *Robert Poley : Prisoner, Spy, and 'Complotter', 1583–9*

13. State Papers (Domestic), vol. ccxxii, no. 13, 7 Jan. 158$\frac{8}{9}$. Examinations of William Yeomans and others before William Fleetwood, Recorder of London.

14. *Ibid.*, no. 14.   Deposition by Richard Ede.
> [Short abstract of both documents in Calendar of State Papers, Domestic, 1581–90, p. 573.]

15. State Papers relating to Scotland and Mary, Queen of Scots.

> C. P., vol. xvi, 10 July 1585 (Thomas Morgan to Mary, Queen of Scots).

16. C. P., vol. xvi, 15 July 1585 (Charles Paget to Mary).

17.   vol. xvii, 18 January 158$\frac{5}{6}$ (Thomas Morgan to Mary and Curll).

18.   21 March 158$\frac{5}{6}$ (Thomas Morgan to Mary).

19.   31 March 1586 (Charles Paget to Mary).

20.   vol. xviii, 27 July 1586 (Mary to Thomas Morgan).

21.   vol. xix, [Aug.] 1586 (Charges against Poley).

22.   [Aug.] 1586 (Confession of Poley).

[Printed in slightly abbreviated form, in modernized spelling, in Calendar of State Papers relating to Scotland and Mary, Queen of Scots, 1547–1603, vol. viii, edited by William K. Boyd.]

23. Lansdowne MSS. 49, f. 63. Letter of Babington to Poley. Other copies in Bodleian, Rawlinson MSS. D 264/1, and B.M. Addit. MSS. 33938, no. 22.

24. MS. Memoirs of William Weston.
[Extracts from the MS. at Stonyhurst College, printed in modernized spelling by John Morris, in *Troubles of our Catholic Forefathers*, and J. H. Pollen in *Mary Queen of Scots and the Babington Plot*, 1922.]

25. Bills of the Lieutenant of the Tower in P.R.O.
   [Numbers E 407/56, nos. 44, 47, 50 printed by Miss de Kalb in *Nineteenth Century and After,* Nov. 1927.]

26. State Papers (France), xvii. 26. Letter from Poley to the Earl of Leicester, February 1587 (?)
   [Transcript, slightly abbreviated, in Cal. of State Papers, Foreign, June 1586–June 1588, pp. 228–9.]

Chapter III. *Marlowe in London : The Charges of Kyd and Baines*

27. MS. Registers of the Stationers' Company.
   [Printed by E. Arber in *A Transcript of the Registers of the Company of Stationers of London, 1554–1640* (1875.)

28. Title-pages of earliest editions of Marlowe's plays and poems.
   [Facsimiles in *The Works of Christopher Marlowe,* ed. C. F. Tucker Brooke, 1910.]

29. Henslowe's MS. *Diary* at Dulwich College.
   [Printed by W. W. Greg, with commentary, 2 vols., 1904.]

30. Middlesex Sessions Roll, 1 October, 31 Elizabeth. Jail-delivery of Christopher Marley of London.
   [Printed by J. C. Jeaffreson in *Middlesex County Records,* vol. i, p. 257.]

147

31. Registers of St. Botolph's Church, East Smithfield.

> [Extracts relating to Humphrey Rowland, 1577–93, printed by J. Leslie Hotson in 'Marlowe Among the Churchwardens', in the *Atlantic Monthly*, July 1926.]

32. King's Bench Controlment Rolls, 1586. Summons to Humphrey Rowland.

> [Printed by Hotson, *Atlantic Monthly*, July 1926.]

33. Thomas Kyd's letters to Sir John Puckering, the Lord Keeper.
Harl. MSS. 6849, f. 218.

> [Transcribed, with facsimile, in *Works of Thomas Kyd*, ed. F. S. Boas, 1901 ; transcribed by F. C. Danchin, *Revue Germanique*, Nov.–Dec. 1913.]

34. Harl. MSS. 6848, f. 154.

> [Transcribed by Ford K. Brown, with some misreadings, in *Times Literary Supplement*, 2 June 1921. Transcribed, with facsimile, in *English Literary Autographs, 1550–1650. Part I. Dramatists*, ed. W. W. Greg, 1925, no. xv. (b).]

35. MS. Fragments of a Socinian treatise quoted in John Proctor's *The Fal of the Late Arrian* (1549). Harl. MSS. 6848, ff. 187–9 (formerly 172–4).

> [Transcribed, with facsimile of f. 189, by Boas, *op. cit.*, and by F. C. Danchin, *op. cit.* W. Dinsmore Briggs (*Studies in Philology*, April 1923) has identified the printed source of the fragments, and has shown what is their right order in 'the Late Arrian's' treatise.]

36. Charges of Richard Baines against Marlowe. Harl. MSS. 6848, ff. 185–6 (formerly 170–1), (original Note). Harl. MSS. 6853, ff. 307–8 (formerly 320–1), (copy sent to Queen Elizabeth).

[Original transcribed with a few omissions by Boas, *op. cit.* Original and copy transcribed in full by Danchin, *op. cit.*]

Chapter IV. *The 'Atheism' of Richard Chomley and Sir Walter Raleigh*

37. 'Remembraunces of wordes and matter againste Ric[hard] Cholmeley.' Harl. MSS. 6848, ff. 190 (formerly 175).

38. Charges against Chomley by an anonymous informer. Harl. MSS. 6848, f. 191 (formerly 176).

39. Letter of Justice Young announcing Chomley's arrest. Harl. MSS. 7002, f. 10.

[Chief parts of these three documents printed by F. S. Boas in *Fortnightly Review*, Feb. 1899, pp. 223–4. Printed in full by Danchin, *op. cit.* 37 and 38 printed by G. B. Harrison, in *Shakespeare's Fellows*, pp. 71–4 (1923).]

40. The Privy Council MS. Register, 13 May and 29 July 1591, and 19 March 159$\frac{2}{3}$. Warrants mentioning Chomley.

[Printed in *Acts of the Privy Council*, ed. Dasent, vols xxi and xxiv.]

41. State Papers (Dom.), Elizabeth, vol. ccxli, no. 19. Letter of Hugh Chomley to Sir Robert Cecil, 19 Jan. 159$\frac{1}{2}$.

[Summarized in Cal. (Dom.), Elizabeth, 1591–4, p. 173, and by Danchin, *Revue Germanique*, Jan.–Feb. 1914, p. 63.]

42. Letter of Earl of Essex concerning Chomley, 13 Nov. 1593.

> [Summarized in Historical MSS. Commission, Fourth Report, p. 330, and by Danchin, *op. cit.*, p. 63.]

43. Depositions of witnesses before the Commission held at Cerne Abbas in Dorset on 21 March 1594, in answer to interrogatories concerning Atheism or Apostacy. Harl. MSS. 6849, ff. 183–90.

> [Extensive extracts printed by J. M. Stone, *The Month*, June 1894, and by F. S. Boas in *Literature*, nos. 147 and 148. Full transcript by Danchin, *op. cit.*, and by G. B. Harrison in Appendix to his edition of *Willobie His Avisa* (1926).

Chapter V. *Marlowe's Death and the Coroner's Inquest*

44. The Privy Council MS. Register, 18 May 1593. Warrant for the arrest of Marlowe.
> [Printed in Dasent, *op. cit.*, vol. xxiv.]

45. Close Rolls, 1339.

46. Exchequer Plea Rolls, 381, 394, and 396. Concerning financial transactions by Ingram Frizer, 1589–95.
> [Summaries of 45 and 46 by J. Leslie Hotson, *The Death of Christopher Marlowe*, pp. 42–57.]

47. Chancery Proceedings, Elizabeth, bundle W. 25, no. 43. Suit of Woodleff *versus* Frizer.

[Printed from the imperfect original document by Hotson, *op. cit.*, pp. 69–71.]

48. Lord Chamberlain, 4/192, p. 267. Bond of Drew Woodleff to Thomas Walsingham, 29 June 1593.

[Summary by Hotson, *op. cit.*, p. 48.]

49. Lansdowne MSS. 44, no. 38. Letter of William Fleetwood to Lord Burleigh, 7 July 1585 mentioning Skeres.

[Mentioned by Sir E. Chambers, *Times Lit. Suppl.* 21 May 1925.]

50. Historical MSS. Commission, Salisbury MSS. v. 139. Arrest of Skeres, 13 March 159$\frac{4}{5}$.

[Summary by Hotson, *op. cit.*, p. 51.]

51. Chancery Miscellanea, bundle 64, file 8, nos. 241 a and 241 b. Writ of *certiorari* to summon the case of Ingram Frizer into Chancery.

52. Inquisition returned by William Danby, Coroner of the Household, in obedience to the writ.

[Both documents printed in full, with English translation, by Hotson, *op. cit.*, pp. 26–34.]

53. Patent Rolls 1401. Enrolment of the Pardon of Ingram Frizer.

[Printed with facsimile by Hotson, *op. cit.*, pp. 34–7 and frontispiece.]

54. Register of St. Nicholas Church, Deptford. Entry of Marlowe's burial, 1 June
1593.
   [Facsimile of part of the page containing the
   entry in J. H. Ingram's *Christopher Marlowe and
   his Associates*, with an erroneous transcription.
   See Hotson, *op. cit.*, pp. 21–2.]

Chapter VI. *The Survivors and the Sequel*

55. Signet Office Docquets: Warrant, 5 Sept.
1603.

56. State Papers (Dom.), Addenda, James I. xl.
46.

57. P.R.O. Index 6801.
Three documents relating to lease of rever-
sion of lands belonging to the Duchy of Lan-
caster to Frizer on behalf of Lady Audrey
Walsingham.
   [Printed by Hotson, *op. cit.*, pp. 49–50.]

58. Subsidies 127/566. Entry concerning
Frizer as an assessor of the parish of Eltham.
   [Summarized by Hotson, *op. cit.*, p. 51.]

59. Eltham Parish Registers. Entries *re* Frizer
in Eltham to August 1627.
   [Summarized by Miss de Kalb, *Times Lit.
   Suppl.* 21 May 1925.]

60. Privy Council MS. Register, 31 July 1601.
Warrant for the removal of Skeres and
Farmer from Newgate to Bridewell.
   [Printed by Dasent, *op. cit.*, xxxii, p. 130.]

61. State Papers (Dom.), Elizabeth, vol. ccxxxviii, no. 140. Deposition of Robert Rutkin, broker, concerning Poley as an agent of Sir Thomas Heneage, April (?) 1591.

   [Summary in Cal. (Dom.), 1591–4, p. 35.]

62. State Papers (Dom.), Elizabeth, vol. ccxlii, no. 25. Letter of Sir Robert Cecil to Sir T. Heneage, 25 May 1592, concerning interview with Poley.

   [Summary, *op. cit.*, p. 223.]

63. State Papers (Dom.), Elizabeth, vol. cclxxv, no. 141. Letter of Poley to Sir R. Cecil, 17 Dec. 1600, concerning Jesuits.

   [Transcribed, in abridged form, and in modernized spelling, in Cal. (Dom.), 1598–1601.]

64. Robert Southwell's *An Humble Supplication to Her Maiestie*, 1595. Includes charges against Poley and Sir F. Walsingham in connexion with the Babington plot.

65. Hatfield MSS. xi. 216, 278, 301, and xii. 230. Poley in July 1601 and July 1602.

   [Summarized by Sir E. Chambers, *Mod. Lang. Rev.*, Jan. 1926.]

66. Gabriel Harvey's *A New Letter of Notable Contents* (1593). Epilogue apparently referring to Marlowe as a victim of the Plague.

67. Thomas Beard's *Theatre of Gods Judgements* (1597).

68. Francis Meres's *Palladis Tamia* (1598).

69. William Vaughan's *The Golden Grove* (1600). 67, 68, and 69 are publications containing contemporary accounts of Marlowe's death.

70. Marlowe's *Hero and Leander* (1598). Edward Blount's dedicatory epistle to Sir Thomas Walsingham.

INDEX

PRINTED IN GREAT BRITAIN AT THE UNIVERSITY PRESS, OXFORD
BY JOHN JOHNSON, PRINTER TO THE UNIVERSITY

Marlowe
AND HIS
CIRCLE
☙
Boas